BOBBY FOSTER

# MACHINES LEARNING FOR BEGINNERS

*A Beginner's Guide to the World of Machine Learning (2023)*

# Contents

# MACHINES FOR BEGINNERS TO LEARN

**AN IN-DEPTH GUIDE TO UNDERSTANDING MACHINE LEARNING.**

**HOW IT FUNCTIONS AND HOW IT INTERACTS WITH ARTIFICIAL INTELLIGENCE AND DEEP LEARNING**

# Introduction

**Artificial intelligence** is a type of machine learning. It enables a computer to acquire knowledge without the need for human intervention or the creation of explicit computer programs that explicitly instruct the computer how to behave. Machine learning is centered on creating dynamic programs that adapt as and when new data becomes available.

The **machine learning method** is comparable to data mining if you've heard of it or have any experience with it. Both methods search for patterns in data, but machine learning takes the data and searches for patterns, learning how to modify the program's actions in response. Data mining pulls data for humans to read.

Both **supervised** and **unsupervised** machine learning algorithms will be mentioned.

While the latter can infer something from a dataset, the former applies prior knowledge to new data. Facebook is a prime illustration. Machine learning is used in the news feed to make your news feed unique to you. If you read or comment on a post from a friend, Facebook will start to show you more of their posts earlier in your feed so you don't have to scroll through to find them. This is accomplished through statistical and predictive analytics, which find trends in your data and use them to populate your news feed.

As you learn more about machine learning, you will find it to be an amazing journey.

You should be inspired to do more by the amazing things you can do with data and the satisfaction you get from creating models that can make reliable predictions. Who knows, you might even create a model that starts a revolution in the field of technology.

The wonder of machine learning is that we work with systems that are programmed to react to our input without requiring us to key in any further instructions beyond what we interact with at the GUI.

We have a lot to learn from this, and there is yet so more to come, given the development of machine learning over the years.

**Machine learning as a field** will give you job opportunities you may not have previously considered. One of the finest things you can anticipate is this. Being an excellent coder is one thing, but mastering the technologies and abilities that will shape the future of computing is quite another.

One step in the correct direction is to pursue a profession in machine learning. One of the most talked-about topics online right now is this. The more time we spend interacting with computers, the more we want to investigate our connections with them and see how far we can take them to free us from as many duties as we can realistically postpone. However, this is a superficial explanation of the appeal of machine learning.

**In-depth,** regardless of whether we try to solve them of our own free will or if we employ computers to take care of them for us, we are dealing with modern issues that suit our technical capacities.

We must find models that can solve these problems within their specific dimensions because the majority of the difficulties we must address through machine learning are thought to be high-dimensional problems.

By using a high-dimensional approach, we may create machine models for problem-solving that are simple to integrate into any or all of the applications we use at work or at home.

Today, most industries have embraced technological development, and machine learning can assist us in building on our current achievements to move toward a better and more seamless future.

**To learn more, continue reading!**

# How does machine learning work?

**In 1959**, Arthur Samuel provided one of the earliest definitions of machine learning. He defined machine learning as a computer's innate ability to learn without the need for programming. **Machine learning,** to put it simply, is the study of strategies and algorithms for automating fixes to issues that can't be resolved through traditional programming. The two stages that make up standard programming are receiving the requirements and putting the design into practice. The specs provide the instructions for what to perform, giving the computer the responsibility for design and execution. Due to the possibility that a machine might not identify the message as intended, traditional programming has proved difficult.

There is a general approach to overcoming these issues in machine learning algorithms. The algorithms can carry out a task without necessarily requiring a complex and precise design because they learn from the labeled data. The level of accuracy is high and they gain knowledge from the information provided. A machine may accurately predict information that is not contained in the set when it "understands" the model of a labeled dataset. Compared to human-made rules, machine learning produces better results. Due to the lack of human bias, ML algorithms incorporate the data points in a dataset, increasing accuracy.

**Machine learning is impossible without data**. The algorithms aid in identifying the data characteristics required for problem solutions. The quality and amount of the data have a big impact on how well we can predict things and learn. Machine learning is now necessary for our daily lives as a result of its improvements to the global economy, health, and other areas of global significance.

**The Workings of Machine Learning**

The development and use of machine-learning algorithms are only a small portion of the overall machine-learning process, which may be broken down into the following steps:

•Define the project's objectives while carefully considering all relevant prior knowledge and subject experience. Goals can easily become vague because there are constantly new things you wish to do but aren't necessarily able to do so.

•A high-quality data set must emerge from the data pre-processing and cleaning. The most important and time-consuming step of the entire endeavor is this one. The training data set must be cleaned up before being fed to the learner system since the more data there is, the more noise it introduces.

•choosing the best learning strategy to suit your project's needs. Given the variety of data models on the market, this procedure is typically quite straightforward.

•As long as the machine learning model can successfully deliver the intended results, the outcomes might or might not require a clear comprehension of the model by human specialists. This depends on the domain the machine learning model is applied to.

•Consolidating and deploying the knowledge or information obtained from the model for usage on an industrial scale is the last phase.

•Up until a practical outcome is attained, the entire cycle from steps 1 through 5 described above is iteratively repeated.

# Category Machine Learning

In practically every aspect of modern life, **computers have become an essential component** of how things are done. Different methods are used to gradually teach computers how to function and perform tasks. Depending on the underlying issues or the expected results, different machine learning paradigms are grouped into taxonomies. These kinds of machine learning enable the computer to discover patterns and regularities that are beneficial in a range of contemporary business and health-related fields. Here are a few learning modalities that are helpful in the machine-learning process.

## Supervised education

When algorithms build a function that converts raw data into desired outputs, supervised learning takes place. One of the most popular paradigms for machine learning is supervised learning. It is simple to understand. Systems from the training dataset may be used to implement the supervised learning process. More than one input and the desired output are present in the training data or examples. The mathematical model's representation of the output is referred to as a regulatory signal. The training example is represented as an array of vectors. The algorithms may be helpful in predicting each name when given data in the form of pictures. When a response is given regarding whether the answers are correct or incorrect, forecasting occurs. The method gives the algorithms an opportunity to gradually learn to approximate in a way that distinguishes between the labels and the examples. The approach makes supervised learning a popular choice when trying to find answers.

As an illustration of how supervised learning streamlines problem-solving, consider the usage of digital recognition.

Because **classification can be used to infer issues,** supervised machine learning is a straightforward method that might be advantageous when the inputs are unclear. When the data are not available, supervised learning takes on more significance as a paradigm. There is always a chance of leaving certain inputs unclear when employing supervised learning. In the presence of such data, the model is useless. However, there will probably be a problem when drawing any conclusions about the outputs when some of the inputs are unavailable.

When training neural networks, one of the simplest and most popular methods is the use of supervised learning.

**Classification** and **regression** are two of the most used supervised learning techniques. When it comes to categorization, supervised learning is used. However, the results could be limited to a set range of values. In a given data set, classification typically involves categorization in order to link new observations into those categories. But when the outputs have a wide range of numerical values within a particular subset, regression is used. The objective in both cases is to make sure that machine learning does the necessary comparisons on how similar or dissimilar a collection of data may be in a particular subset using a specific set of training instances. The best-case scenarios in these data set guarantee that the algorithms can identify the class labels for all occurrences that are not visible within that subgroup.

## Unsupervised Education

Through unsupervised cluster analysis, machines may learn.

The method entails using a set of input-based data, which is required for the creation of a structure. An illustration of unsupervised learning is the clustering of data points. The test data in unsupervised learning does not have labels and is not classified in any way, as opposed to supervised learning.

**Unsupervised learning concentrates** on the similarities rather than responding to input. The technique looks for potential commonalities in a piece of data and uses those commonalities to create patterns. In essence, this means that the objective is to give a computer a task to learn how to do something without offering a rational strategy to accomplish this task. As a result, the unsupervised method is more difficult and complex than the supervised method. This strategy entails using rewards to recognize the accomplishment of the tasks without necessarily giving clear instructions on how to get the desired outcomes.

The **unsupervised approach's goal** is more in line with the decision-making process than it is with just classifying these facts. Unsupervised learning teaches the agent how to act or react to tasks using a reward or punishment system that has been developed over time.

Without prior knowledge of the expected results, a computer eventually learns how to navigate past orders. This strategy could be difficult and time-consuming. Unsupervised learning, however, can be effective because it relies on trial and error, which can lead to discoveries. Unsupervised learning relies on an aspect of innovation because it does not take into account any previously classified data.

Backgammon, one of the most challenging chess games ever created, is a common example used to illustrate the application of unsupervised learning. As a result of playing against themselves repeatedly, a number of unsupervised programs eventually outperformed the original game format in terms of understanding the rules and structure. What actually happened was that these programs gradually learned fresh ideas and methods for playing the game, which marked a crucial turning point in how the game was designed. Clustering is another guise for unsupervised learning. In this method, the overarching goal is not to maximize a fundamental utility function but rather to identify commonalities among the set of data. Without a set of pre-classified data, the approach enables the process of deriving meaning from a collection of data. The clustered approach makes the assumption that the established clusters will eventually display specific similarities that correspond to an intuitive categorization. Thus, examples that convey meaning can be developed using the groups discovered, and new models can be built using these clusters.

In a world where most data sets are unlabeled, the unsupervised learning method is essential. This indisputable fact makes it essential to have sophisticated algorithms that can use terabytes of unlabeled data and make sense of it. Unsupervised learning will become an important topic of focus in a variety of situations in the future. Future applications of unsupervised learning will be crucial in the field of recommender systems. The recommender system makes it simple to categorize and suggest content based on common preferences because it enables a clear link to relationships.

The **use of unsupervised learning** to support recommender systems may be seen in YouTube. The method enables the viewer to observe the total number of viewers for a particular video and provides recommendations for comparable videos that these viewers have also viewed in an effort to match shared interests. Recommender systems may be useful for social media platforms like Facebook as they try to group individuals into a particular cluster. Large corporations may also profit from the unsupervised learning approach by analyzing the purchasing patterns of the market's diverse consumer base. Unsupervised learning can help segment these data sets into groups that correspond to the requirements for particular products or services.

## Reward-Based Learning

Because reinforcement learning rarely assumes knowledge of an accurate mathematical model, it is helpful when the exact models are unrealistic. The strategy focuses on the optimal operation of machines to maximize a certain feature of cumulative reward. In contemporary studies, the use of reinforcement learning is investigated from a behavioral psychology perspective. Thus, the method operates by interacting with its surroundings.

As we just mentioned, supervised learning relies on previous examples to function. The user's interaction with the environment in the reinforcement learning scenario reveals a distinction between the two methodologies.

The **use of reinforcement learning** in artificial intelligence is a sign of the machines' capacity to pick up new skills and adapt to new tasks through interactions with their immediate surroundings. Based on their observation of the contextual environment, the algorithms modify their behavior to do particular actions. The behavioral pattern in response to environmental stimuli is a sign of the learning process, which has come to be associated with artificial intelligence.

Every action in reinforcement learning has an immediate impact on the operational context, and this response gives the machine a chance to get feedback, which is essential for the learning process. The use of time-dependent sequences or labels is frequently used in reinforcement learning. The relationship between the agent and the environmental context affects the outcomes in the reinforcement learning scenario. Following that, the agent is given a set of tasks that directly affect the environment. The approach then approves a particular reinforcement signal, which, depending on the task and the desired outcome, either sends negative or positive feedback.

In a crude manner, if a reinforcement learning algorithm is introduced into a certain situation, it might first make glaring errors. By rewarding positive conduct and penalizing negative behavior, reinforcement learning aims to make sure that this system receives timely feedback on its errors. As a result, the algorithm starts to comprehend that positive behaviors draw rewards through direct input from the environment. The algorithm is allowed to make mistakes throughout this machine-learning process, and then this strategy is used to help the algorithm forget the techniques that may have caused these errors.

Due to the behavior-driven nature of the reinforcement learning methodology, there will be multiple applications for the technique in a variety of sectors, including the development of simulation-based optimization. Reinforcement learning, which conditions a machine using behavioral patterns, draws on significant findings in the fields of neuroscience and psychology. Behavioral learning has played a key role in the development of autonomous vehicles as well as other fields like game theory. The majority of computer games, including Mario, may be helpful in evaluating the relationship between the environment and the agent. In a game where points serve as reinforcement techniques, the agent can accumulate points and advance to new levels. The algorithm eventually develops a pattern thanks to the application of reinforcement, where the levels or points serve as a gauge of reinforcement.

## Machine learning that is semi-supervised

When there is a little amount of labeled data and a large number of unlabeled data, semi-supervised learning algorithms must be used. The technique makes use of both labeled and unlabeled data. Thus, the programmer searches for patterns using both data types. The associations that target variables are based on the inferred models, and it is simple to recognize and examine the data instances. The method is referred to as semisupervised learning since it makes sense of data from both labeled and unlabeled samples.

As a result, semi-supervised learning is a combination of supervised and unsupervised learning strategies. Because semi-structured data does not adhere to the formal structuring of data models, it is used in this situation. The semi-supervised approach's usage of tags and other indicators helps to separate the semantic components. When there aren't enough examples to build an accurate model, this is crucial. Semi-structured models frequently make perfect sense when there aren't enough resources or capabilities to expand the pool of available data instances.

**According to researchers,** a variety of functional disciplines, such as webpage classification and speech recognition, benefit from using the semi-supervised learning approach. Across the board, scientists have endorsed the use of this method; more recently, the field of genetic sequencing has done the same. Even when such labels are left blank in the current human-inputted labels, the application of semi-supervised algorithms enables the recognition of the nature of individual web pages in a given environment. These approaches have a higher likelihood of being effective and being used across a wider range of operational settings and domains since they permit the incorporation of both labeled and unlabeled data. Therefore, a key benefit of using this technique is the ability to increase the training data by utilizing both data sets.

The method allows for the labeling of the designated data, and then it employs the trained model to categorize the other data in accordance with the particular model. In some cases, you could encounter circumstances where you have a large amount of data with a known consequence and another set of data that is unknown. The procedure can take advantage of the existing data models by using semi-supervised machine learning to create a labeling sequence that will work for the remaining data sets. As a result, when compared to other models, this method offers the greatest alternative because it saves time and significantly cuts down on the total amount of resources needed to achieve the desired result.

In a contemporary environment where unlabeled data is likely to outweigh labeled data throughout the classification process, the development of an appropriate function when employing semi-supervised techniques may be a significant solution. The most current example in the modern world is the employment of semi-supervised approaches for spam identification and detection from standard messages. Otherwise, it would be impossible to use human knowledge to filter through such messages. Using semi-supervised approaches aids in addressing the high dimensionality issue that frequently interferes with the classification process.

The employment of self-training strategies is one of the most popular semi-supervised learning techniques. The method enables the class to go through a learning process initially utilizing a tiny labeled data set. The research's classifier is then utilized to categorize a variety of unlabeled data. However, the need to address the problem of selecting highly consistent predictions still raises significant concerns. The second method that works well in semi-supervised processes is modeling, specifically generative models. Unlabeled samples are at the center of the model's repeated approach, which underlies all of its operations. Comparing models that are derived from this data to models that are derived from training instances, the technique shows a better acceptable performance in the case of the models from this information. The interactive training strategy is one of the repetitive methods commonly used in generative methods.

The co-training strategy, in which only a very small portion of the data is labeled, is the third typical method used when using the semi-supervised algorithm. The context frequently contains a sizable amount of unlabeled data, which could make classification more difficult.

**Using labeled samples**, the techniques enable running a different rating for each view. One can also use the margin-based approach when using the semi-skilled learning strategy. The technique focuses on growing the support vector machine, which could significantly affect the decrease in overall margin costs. Semi-supervised learning can offer a crucial chance to save costs and shorten the time spent on classification. The recent discovery of deep learning, which will essentially solve all the fundamental issues with semi-supervised learning, is an illustration of this progressive achievement.

The ideal strategy for dealing with semi-supervised models is to be aware of the shortcomings of each choice. The self-training approach is the most straightforward because it can be applied to practically all categories. According to the majority of semi-supervised hardliners, this iterative strategy is essentially always used when dealing with classifications. This method's only drawback is that it doesn't provide much information on convergence. The truth is that self-training may reinforce mistakes, a problem that could reduce the option's effectiveness. Some of the most accurate forecasts, which are typically noticeably nearer to the answers, can be found in generative models. The method is also becoming increasingly important as a source of answers for problems relating to data system knowledge and issues that arise when interacting with such structures. The failure to address the underlying classification issues when doing research is a concern that this technique also raises. The biggest worry is the apparent restriction in genitive models when balancing unlabeled and labeled data when the latter is constrained. When errors are likely to harm the model, generative models may be concerned about the possibility of making mistakes.

### Learning Features

The different features that may have an impact on the result must be recognized and determined while carrying out a specific machine learning assignment. When given a task, feature learning is the collection of techniques that enables the identification of the necessary representation of data samples in the process of achieving the desired machine learning results. When performing the task of classification, a typical example is the requirement to determine the appropriate description of the data. When the in-question data is linearly inseparable, the use of feature learning as a feasible machine learning approach is very important.

Depending on the classification goal, feature learning may be supervised or unsupervised.

Given the similar meaning of both terms, it is fair to use representative learning to explain feature learning. The strategy aims to preserve the information in the data examples while also changing the data to make it useful for the process of meaning creation. The method enables the computer to learn and utilize the data for a variety of jobs and functionality. Labeled data input is used to facilitate supervised feature learning. The employment of multilayer perception or supervised neural networks is a sign that feature learning is being used. For instance, supervised neural networks make use of computational ease to accomplish the desired goals. Unsupervised feature learning can be helpful in locating the appropriate representation while carrying out machine learning tasks.

In order to fulfill some machine learning duties, the method entails mapping raw data into a clear description of the same data.

**The most important benefit of deep learning** is that the algorithms concentrate on learning high-level properties from the given data in an incremental manner. The method always works since it gets rid of difficult feature extraction. The use of feature learning in the process of meeting the established goals also has a crucial advantage in that it lessens the requirement for domain knowledge because this method makes sure that the computers can learn advanced degrees of data mining and classification.

The goal of the unsupervised feature learning approach is to learn from unlabeled data by gaining insight into the low dimensional properties present in such data sets. The idea of semi-supervised data sets, where learning takes place through unlabeled data sets, is frequently incorporated into the model. The knowledge gained from these data sets is then employed to solve the gaps in a supervised context with labeled data.

The feature learning method presents a number of choices. One of the methods is K-means clustering. When considering a set of n vectors during the vector-quantization process, the k-means algorithm is used. K is the clustering of these vectors into clusters under k.

Each vector is made to fit into the groups that suggest a notion of having the closest mean by the subgroups. The method is applied in the clustering of unlabeled sets of data examples. Each sample that has the k-means as being the most similar to the data examples is added k binary as part of the operation.

The principal component analysis method may be used in conjunction with feature learning. When attempting to solve the dimensional problem, which is a frequent issue, the technique is helpful. The issue becomes apparent when the sample data vector is subtracted from the example data mean. In the context of PCA, the p vectors are linear functions that may be generated using straightforward techniques.

**Although** this method is the most popular feature learning technique, it has a number of drawbacks that could have an impact on the results of linear learning. The approach's first drawback is that it operates on the presumption that, among observed variances, the most significant one serves as the foundation for shared interest. Since this is not always the case, the direction with the greatest variety of variations may not warrant the greatest amount of attention. The method's tendency to just use or concentrate on the first two moments of the data set has also been considered a weakness of the strategy. The predictability of the data distribution in a particular data example may frequently be directly impacted by the emphasis on the first two factors. The PCA may only be used in situations where the various data vectors coincide with a potentially extremely restrictive characteristic.

**Additionally,** local linear embedding may be used while the feature learning process is being carried out. In the process of non-linear learning, the technique entails the reconstruction of high-dimensional data using low-dimensional variables from the original data sets. The technique aims to extract from a given set of input data the intrinsic geometric properties of a neighborhood. The LLE is a more efficient method for carrying out feature learning when compared to the PCA. Independent component analysis may be incorporated into the feature learning strategy. The technique creates a data representation that makes use of a weighted sum inside the larger data set by using distinct non-Gaussian components. However, all of these methods work to make sure that the variables and attributes in a data set are easily determined, allowing predictions to be made in a specific data example. The ability to classify and forecast data even when they are linearly separate, however, emphasizes the importance of feature learning in ML.

# Industries and Sectors Using Machine Learning

The **corporate** and **political worlds** both use machine learning. Since this is meant to be a generalized method that can be used to apply computing power, the applications are numerous and diverse. After briefly discussing a few concrete instances, let's gain an understanding of the potential applications of machine learning across a range of industries and social groups.

## Government

The government is quite interested in machine learning, as you might expect. All levels of government, from local to national, have a stake in a given issue. In fact, machine learning is being used by a large number of centralized governments around the globe for both good and harmful reasons.

**Machine learning** is used by the military in all of its activities. This will assist the military in creating more effective machinery that can function with little to no assistance from humans. This can be viewed as a benefit or as something that might give rise to ethical questions, depending on the use.

As we've seen, machine learning has been utilized by Southwest Airlines and other businesses like UPS to pinpoint problems that result in lost time, fuel, and money. At first look, the U.S. military might not appear to be all that comparable to UPS and Southwest Airlines, but keep in mind that in addition to fighting wars, the military is a logistics and transportation behemoth. The military must be able to transfer large numbers of personnel by air, sea, or land, as well as heavy equipment from one site to another with the utmost efficiency in order to maintain supplies for troops in far-off areas.

In the military, machine learning is being used to enhance logistics and transportation in order to save money on fuel, cut down on idle time, and increase the effectiveness of the movement of personnel and goods.

For the military, target recognition is a crucial use of machine learning. Soldiers can find and follow potential targets with the use of machine learning. This can lessen the possibility of causing civilian casualties while increasing the accuracy and efficiency of real-time targeting operations. The model can learn during the training phase by being shown data about prior adversary behaviors and movements.

**Cybersecurity is one area where machine learning is proving to be useful**. Machine learning-trained algorithms can assist in stopping cyberattacks, detecting bogus attempts to access a network, and even launching counterattacks. As a subfield of artificial intelligence, machine learning systems used in cyber security are capable of acting independently. Machine learning is being used to improve cybersecurity at all levels of government and both inside and outside the military.

Another federal agency that has boosted the use of machine learning in its operations recently is the Internal Revenue Service. The IRS is particularly interested in utilizing machine learning to assist in the detection of fraud and identity theft. Additionally, fraud cases' historical data can be examined in order to find patterns that can be used to forecast where fraud will occur in the future.

Machine learning is being used by the Centers for Disease Control for many different objectives. One suggestion, for instance, is to analyze epidemics using machine learning. This might make it easier for healthcare professionals to spot outbreaks and take appropriate action when warranted. When patterns of cases appearing at different hospitals could be used to identify when an epidemic is forming and forecast its future course, data is frequently decentralized and processed only after the fact in the current system.

**Additionally,** local governments are utilizing machine learning to improve service delivery and stop fraud and theft. Police agencies can utilize problematic machine learning to scan faces in a crowd and identify criminals they may be looking for or to scan license plates and follow movements.

Machine learning is being used by some local governments to better allocate resources. This can be done for any duty carried out by the local government, including road maintenance, sewage cleaning and upkeep, the distribution of police patrols among different neighborhoods, and restaurant inspections. Criminal activity can also be modeled using machine learning. Once trained, the algorithm could predict where future crimes would occur, what kinds of crimes they would be, and the number of police resources that should be allocated to each region by learning from historical patterns of criminal behavior.

Using machine learning to forecast the conduct of persons who have been detained in a different field in which municipal, state, and federal agencies are interested. This is highly contentious and might raise constitutional concerns in the US, as you can guess. It would calculate the probability that a certain person will appear for a trial if released based on the data points linked with that person. The system might suggest that a defendant be held without bail or even allow for release on their own recognizance. If the subject is found guilty, the system can estimate the likelihood that they will commit new crimes based on an analysis of the data points related to them.

As you can see, the government uses machine learning in numerous additional applications and across a wide range of ministries. Although there is some controversy surrounding these applications, governments will attempt to use them because of their power. So anticipate hearing a lot about this in the future.

## Monetary services

You won't be surprised to find that banks, mortgage firms, and all other sorts of financial service providers use machine learning to improve and, from their perspective, increase the efficiency of their operations. Although machine learning has a seemingly limitless number of uses in the financial sector, fraud detection is the first one where it is heavily utilized. When it seems like someone is creating a fake account, using an account for fraudulent activity, or using identity theft to obtain financial services, this can be used to identify the situation. The use of a debit card in a manner that is consistent with the patterns found when cards are stolen is a straightforward example that might resonate with some of our readers. If you have ever had your card blocked even if you have it and are only using it to do errands and make purchases with your debit card, you are well aware of the dangers associated with machine learning gone wrong.

Credit checks and loan approval are two other aspects of financial services that have been dominated by machine learning. The necessity of speaking with a loan officer is quickly coming to an end, and in some circumstances, it has already happened. This is actually one of the simplest uses of machine learning because the algorithm can be quickly trained using the reams of historical data gathered from the financial activities of tens of millions of people. This can effectively train the algorithm to identify the loan applicants who are most likely to default in the current pool of applicants. Mistakes will inevitably occur since, as we just established, these systems will never be flawless.

## Shipping and Transportation

We've already mentioned how Southwest and other airlines have used machine learning to more efficiently distribute their resources and prevent needless waste of fuel and time. The same methods employed by aircraft can be applied to haulage and shipping as well as any application involving mass transit. For instance, machine learning can assist a trucking company in making the best use of its resources to save fuel expenses and cut down on driver idle time. By functioning autonomously and more effectively than a person, machine learning increases the effectiveness of shipping by being able to decide how to classify commodities for shipping and what goods should be put on what ships. We must also consider the prospect that eventually self-driving cars, trains, and ships may reach their destinations back and forth without the need for human intervention. It's unclear how much the possible applications will be used on a wide scale because there are undoubtedly many legal and ethical concerns that go along with them.

### oil, gas, and mining

The oil and gas sector as well as mining both directly benefit from machine learning. It can be used, for example, to look for new resources or energy sources. When looking for potential locations for experimental drilling, this can help businesses become far more effective. They can swiftly exclude locations that are most likely to be less promising by using machine learning. The transportation and storage sectors of the mining, oil, and gas industries are significant. Once more, machine learning's capacity to boost the effectiveness of logistics and transportation can be very beneficial to these sectors. Additionally, machine learning can be used to maximize storage efficiency and distribute information more effectively. These applications carry some risk; occasionally, a human geologist may be able to identify a suitable location for exploratory drilling that a machine learning-based system would have missed. Overall, though, the program will be more successful and efficient.

### online and retail marketing

These days, everyone is talking about the phenomenon of online adverts that seem to read your mind. These systems' underlying technology is based on machine learning. You will encounter shoe adverts wherever you go if you're looking for a new pair of shoes. It's unclear whether this always works because the algorithms can't tell why someone is looking at anything online.

These systems, if they haven't already, are probably connected to your offline behavior at "brick and mortar" stores as well as your online conduct. Privacy advocates are dissatisfied in this particular area, but it is unclear where this will end up. However, it will be very challenging to stop the practice because it gives marketers strong results and generates a lot of advertising revenue.

## Healthcare

Healthcare is an intriguing industry where machine learning is beginning to make a difference. Medical professionals frequently need to use their problem-solving and interpretation abilities, yet a lot of medicine is rule-based, with therapies that can be quickly identified by machine learning systems. You may envisage how a system could be educated by looking at databases that have information about a lot of people who have high blood pressure and researching the medications that doctors prescribed. A machine learning system can easily mimic this behavior and might even perform better because it can analyze a person's traits and tease out patterns from huge patient databases to look for patterns that correlate one treatment over another with success, or conversely, with side effects. When prescriptions for illnesses are essentially routine, one can imagine a system where they are written entirely automatically. Additionally, oral diabetic medications could be prescribed, as well as antibiotics for sinus infections and sore throats. This would increase the overall effectiveness of the healthcare system and free up doctors to engage in other endeavors that make greater use of their skills.

**In more sophisticated circumstances,** machine learning can also serve as a doctor's helper. A clinician might miss something that an algorithm can identify, resulting in more precise diagnoses and treatments.

Intriguingly, artificial intelligence and machine learning are being used to build surgical robots that can either support a doctor or perhaps take their place. This is undoubtedly a more sophisticated use of the technology. In the future, it could be used to help bring medicine to remote areas where there are fewer hospitals and doctors.

In a sizable healthcare facility, machine learning can also be used to assist with staffing, appointment scheduling, and patient distribution. As you have probably already guessed, machine learning is excellent for creating systems that handle and resolve logistical issues like these. This has the potential to save a lot of money over time, given the high level of inefficiency in the healthcare system.

# Normative Algorithms

**Educated machines that can learn?** That sounds almost frightening. But it isn't because "machine learning" actually refers to techniques that should make algorithms more effective.

## Learning through data adaptation

Machine learning is used in the majority of artificial intelligence (AI) applications. This method is frequently used in image, audio, and text recognition programs, diagnostic and translation software, and programs created to evaluate risks or determine the likelihood of future clients.

The majority of algorithms always act in the same way: the same data yields the same outcome. The so-called learning algorithms fall under a unique group. They modify their functioning in response to the data they handle.

*Consequently, this procedure is known as machine learning.*

## Optimize outcomes: a training issue

The **goal of machine learning** is to **increase the accuracy of algorithmic results**. How much data is weighted when an algorithm determines a result is one facet of "learning". For instance, it specifies that some facts or information need to have a higher influence on the result than others. Most people handle this task. For instance, an algorithm may randomize the weighting before selecting the variant that yields the best outcomes. Humans frequently have a significant influence on machine learning. Consequently, it is common to refer to algorithms as being "trained."

So the goal is to enhance the output of an algorithm. In some instances, this algorithmic improvement is automated. This is helpful for recurring tasks like estimating the likelihood that a customer will purchase from an online retailer.

Here, an algorithm is **"trained"** to identify from data certain behavior patterns that point to a purchase as accurately as possible. Such information might consist of things like the amount of time spent on a product page, where the mouse pointer moved, or how many times related products were seen. The AI may then independently verify which instances a projected purchase actually took place. The weighting of the gathered data is then changed in preparation for the following probability computation.

Limits of machine learning lead to imbalance

The quality and type of the data are just as crucial to machine learning as their quantity. The effectiveness of an AI program is impacted by outdated, inaccurate, incorrect, or inappropriate data. The results are distorted when data sets are used that leave the application area unfinished or just partially complete.

For instance, if an AI is trained exclusively on data from a particular demographic group and is tasked with evaluating the development of disease symptoms, it may be assessing reality; it's probable that the conclusions won't be very helpful to groups with different living conditions. As a result, machine learning practitioners should be able to discern precisely when and how the algorithms might be applied in a useful manner. Recognizing their limitations is another aspect of this, particularly when it comes to something as important as human health.

Machine learning, at its most fundamental level, is the use of several preprogrammed algorithms to gather and evaluate data in order to identify potential outcomes that fall within a reasonable range. The system learns and adjusts when fresh data is received by these algorithms, enhancing performance.

**<u>Some common algorithms are:</u>**

**<u>Regular Regression</u>**

Of all the machine learning-related algorithms, linear regression is arguably the most well-known. Finding the path that best reflects the linear trend, or in other words, finding the line that best fits the situation, is the basic tenet of this approach. It presupposes that the various input variables have a linear connection to one another.

The procedure is known as a simple linear regression when there is only one input variable (x), but it is known as a multiple linear regression when there are numerous input variables.

A linear algorithm's fundamental nature is to combine a certain set of input variables, with the result being a real, predictable output. Both the input and the output values must be numerical in these circumstances.

A single scale factor, or coefficient, is assigned to each input value. The capital Greek letter Beta (B) designates it. The line gains an additional coefficient, giving it the ability to travel up or down a two-dimensional plot line.

The bias coefficient is used to describe this.

 **Y + B0 +B1*X**

A hyper-plane is what you deal with when there are higher dimensions and more inputs are involved.

When a coefficient is zero, the influence of the input variable is canceled out.

Situations like this one are pertinent when you require a way to control how the neural network adapts and changes. There are numerous applications for linear regression.

- •When estimating coefficients from a single input variable, simple linear regression can be used. It enables you to compute statistical features like means, deviations, correlations, and covariance that were retrieved from input data.
- •When you need to estimate the values of the coefficients, and you have more than one input, you should utilize ordinary least squares. It performs the estimations by treating the data as a matrix and using linear algebraic operations.
- •When processing the coefficient values with numerous inputs, gradient descent is employed. For each coefficient, random values are used to make it operate. The learning rate is then computed by adding the **input** and **output** values' sum of mistakes. The results are then updated using this as a scale in an effort to lower the rate of error.
- •Regularization is the last step. These are additions designed to reduce error rates during the training phase, but they are also used to reduce the model's complexity.

When you have binary classification issues, logistic regression is a fairly popular solution. When this occurs, there are only two possible solutions. It is sometimes referred to as dichotomy and is effective for solving issues that call for a true/false or yes/no response.

You must first have a thorough understanding of linear regression before you can properly appreciate logistic regression. You must choose the ideal line as an analyst to depict a particular trend. Finding an equation that provides the best direct feature and solves the regression problem is necessary for this.

The **least squares method is typically employed,** with the goal of reducing the distance between the line and the training set of data.

The system just searches for a line that is "nearest" to all of the supplied data.

A **special kind of algorithm called the generalized linear model** includes logistic regression. In contrast to linear regression, your goal is to identify a model that most closely approximates the final value of the outcome or variable. Although there is no specific value to predict because you are solving a binary problem, keep that in mind. There are only two conceivable outcomes. Actually, you're looking for the possibility that one outcome will actually happen.

**What would be a good problem for linear regression to address? How much snow will we get this year?**

The following issues would be resolved by logical regression: Will it snow tomorrow?

**Choice Trees**

A model is more frequently classified and labeled in a tree structure using decision tree methods. They are regarded by many analysts as excellent tools that can provide them with accurate and trustworthy output data.

**Decision trees** are **straightforward** to read and comprehend. In fact, using them will enable you to clearly understand why specific classifiers are required in order to reach a conclusion. This algorithm is definitely the best one to start out with if you're new to programming.

These algorithms all take the same exact method, which is to divide the data into as few subsets as possible (those that only include one group of results). Depending on the available predictors, the data is broken up. Then they combine all subsets belonging to the same class. They will keep doing this until they have the smallest possible amount of data.

Once this is done, predicting the behavior that will occur is very simple. This kind of forecast is relatively easy to make.

The system only follows the path that corresponds to the provided predictions. It will result in the subset containing all of the affirmative responses.

## Stability Vector Machines

SVMs, or support vector machines, are algorithms that can be employed as tools of war. SVMs, in contrast to the others, stated, can produce results that are significantly more accurate than any of the others we've discussed.

This kind of method is incredibly complicated and makes use of some of the trickiest mathematical formulae. SVMs can only process extremely tiny amounts of datasets because of their particular complexity. Therefore, it is likely that SVM is not the best choice if the initial training data is too large.

Classifications are performed using SVMs. It looks for the best line to draw between all the many classes of data the system might be taking into account. Simply said, it seeks out the largest data separation (or margin) between all the various groupings or possible subsets.

## Simple Bayes

The Naive Bayes algorithm solves classification problems using statistical modeling. It is rather straightforward, but when applied correctly, it can offer very exact solutions. When compared to support vector machines, arguably the most complex of all the algorithms in use today, it is very scalable.

The foundation of Naive Bayes is the Bayes Theorem, which makes the supposition that "all predictors are independent of each other."

This algorithm does not keep any data in its memory; nevertheless, it studies and evaluates the training data and makes use of that understanding to adjust as necessary.

All predictors are interdependent in reality, but Naive Bayes treats them all as separate entities that are not related to one another.

Each predictor is given a probability when the system evaluates the data, placing them together in a single class that is unrelated to any other attributes. The "class predictor probability" is what is used to describe this.

Think about how it might assess and identify the class of a particular fruit as an example. It might conduct an initial analysis and discover that the fruit is red. The program then consults its database of fruit information to ascertain the existence of red apples, cherries, and strawberries.

It finds that the form is round when it examines the following categorization, and shape. Strawberries are not round, but apples, oranges, and peaches are. It will then consider the diameter size. The fruit in this forecast has a diameter of 3". Now, this might be an orange, a peach, an apple, or a pomegranate. After taking into account each attribute, it will assign a percentage of likelihood that the fruit belongs to one of many classes, with the class with the highest percentage being the one most likely to meet the predetermined criteria. The pattern can resemble this:

- likelihood of an apple 80%
- chance of orange10%
- Chance of Strawberries 5%, 10%,
- etc.

One of the first things you learn about algorithms if you've studied them previously is that there are hundreds, if not thousands, of them.

Depending on the algorithm you apply, machines can learn. Machine learning is incredibly likely and not just likely with the correct algorithm.

# Analysis of Regression

**linear regressive**

**One of the most used methods of predictive analysis is linear regression. Two**

**things are involved in linear regression:**

•Are the outcome variables accurately predicted by the predictor variables?

•Which specific variables are crucial determinants of the result variable, and to

what extent does it affect it?

**Varying names**

The dependent variable in the regression has numerous names.

The terms outcome variable, criteria variable, and several more are examples of names. The exogenous variable or repressors are other names for the independent variable.

**the purposes of regression analysis**

•Forecasting trends

•Identify the predictors' strength

•Speculate on a result

**Separating regression**

Regression can exist in two basic states: **linear regression** and **multiple regression.** Nevertheless, there are various techniques for handling and analyzing complex data. An independent variable is used in linear regression to predict the result of a dependent variable. Multiple regression, on the other hand, uses two or more independent variables to aid in the prediction of a result.

Because it is used to forecast sales of a particular product or company based on historical sales and GDP growth among many other factors, regression is very helpful to financial and investment institutions. One of the most widely used regression models in finance is the capital price model.

**Deciding which regression model is best**

Making the appropriate linear regression model choice can be challenging and complex. It cannot be made simpler by attempting to model it with sample data. This section examines some of the most often-used statistical approaches for selecting models, discusses potential difficulties, and provides helpful guidance for choosing the best regression model.

It always starts with a researcher who wants to deepen the connection between predictors and the response variable. The research team assigned the task of conducting the investigation essentially measures many factors but only includes a small number in the model. The analysts will work to eliminate the extraneous factors and apply the ones that accurately reflect the relationship. The analysts keep creating new models throughout time.

**How to use statistics to select the most effective regression model**

The sort of variables you wish to test as well as other variables that can affect the response must be taken into account if you want a great regression model.

R-squared modifications and predicted R-squared.

Higher modified and anticipated R-squared values are desirable for your model. The statistics below assist in removing important R-squared-related problems.
●When a new term enhances the model, the adjusted R squared rises.

•Predicted R-squared is a component of cross-validation, which aids in defining how your model can generalize to other data sets.

## For the Predictors, P-values

A low value of P indicates statistically significant terms in regression. The practice of including all potential predictors in a model is referred to as "reducing the model."
incremental regression

This automated method can pick significant predictors that were discovered during the model-building process' exploratory phases.

## Real-World Obstacles

The best model can be chosen using a variety of statistical methods. However, difficulties persist.

- When the study measures the variables, the best model results.
- The type of data collection procedure could lead the sample data to be atypical. When you handle samples, a false positive and false negative process takes place.
- If you work with enough models, you'll find variables that are statistically significant but are simply randomly connected.
- P-values can vary based on the particular model terms used.
- Research has shown that stepwise regression and the best subset regression cannot choose the right model.

## The proper Regression Model Theory to use

Perform research on it and incorporate it into your model. It's crucial to come up with suggestions for the most critical variables before you begin regression analysis.

The process of gathering data is made easier when something is developed based on results from other people.

## Complexity

You may believe that complicated models are required for complex situations. That is untrue, however, as research demonstrates that even a straightforward model is capable of making precise predictions. The simplest model is probably the best option once there is a model with the same explanatory power. Simply begin with a straightforward model and progressively increase its complexity.

### How to determine a predictive model's accuracy

You can compute the accuracy of your model in a variety of ways. Some of these techniques consist of:

• The dataset is split into a training and test data set. Then, use the test set as a holdout sample to build the model based on the training set and evaluate it using the test data. The next step is to compare the actual values to the projected values in order to calculate the error using metrics like the "Mean Absolute Percent Error" (MAPE). You have a great model if your MAPE is lower than 10%.

• Calculating the "Confusion Matrix" to the computer's False Positive Rate and False Negative Rate is another way. A person will have the option to approve or reject the model based on these measures. It becomes a crucial stage of your decision whether to reject or accept the model when you take the cost of the inaccuracies into account.

• You can also utilize the Lift Chart, the Receiver Operating Characteristic Curve (ROC), or the Area Under the Curve (AUC) to determine whether to accept or reject a model.

# Machine Learning's Advantages

**Why should you have a conversation about machine learning now?** If you have recently engaged in conversations on machine learning, artificial intelligence, and big data, you must have picked up a few tips and have a general knowledge of the topics covered.

Many users of machine learning engage in activity without fully understanding what they are doing. The spam filter in our emails is among the best instances of machine learning that we unintentionally use.

Ever wonder how the spam filter distinguishes between legitimate emails and spam emails automatically? This is machine learning at work, improving your life.

In this section, we will discuss some of the **factors that make machine-learning knowledge crucial**, particularly in a world that is rapidly automating. Every day, data scientists and other professionals in the industry work with enormous amounts of data.

When put via the proper algorithms, this data can be used to inform crucial choices. Algorithms are designed in a way that allows them to learn from data sets, ultimately increasing the effectiveness of some of the judgments we make.

Insofar as the business community is concerned, machine learning models are crucial because they enable decision-making that is correct without the need for extensive staff involvement. By doing this, redundant business processes are reduced.

**Let's look at another example** using a typical Google search query. Any outcome could be found with a simple search. To ensure that your results are pertinent or as close to what you need as feasible, Google uses special algorithms that are active in the background. It would be ludicrous to find results for properties in Antananarivo if you are looking for them in Houston.

Results that are sufficiently relevant to your demands are shown by the Google algorithms. This data is based on a wide range of characteristics and variables, such as your geographical location at the time of the request, your browsing history, or even the online activities of other users who may be looking for the same keywords as you.

As a result, machine learning employs algorithms to do particular jobs without necessarily needing your explicit instructions. Based on your interactions and experiences with the system, the outcome is presented to you. And it doesn't stop there. Your receipt of the information transforms it into a knowledge foundation for the system. The system absorbs this information and improves itself to provide even better results more quickly the next time you need them. Here are a few explanations of why machine learning is crucial.

## Making Decisions

You constantly have to make split-second decisions in the commercial world. Making the proper choice at the right moment frequently makes the difference between a successful and unsuccessful business decision. We live in a world where data and information are used extensively in corporate activities. The right information must be obtained by decision-makers from the appropriate sources at the appropriate time.

Smart business involves more than just receiving accurate information at the appropriate moment. While doing so, intelligent technology use is also important.

Businesses can employ machine learning to transform their data access into an intelligent knowledge base that, when used to take action, produces meaningful intelligence.

The data gathered from these systems is then transformed into routine business operations, assisting the business in managing operational activities in a way that will eventually enable it to both respond to market demands and meet its own expectations as stated in its business objectives. In the long run, businesses are consequently in an excellent position to stay ahead of the competition and increase their potential in real-time thanks to machine learning.

## Task Management Streamlining

The removal of pointless manual tasks from business processes is one area where machine learning has been successful. If you examine the development of industrial automation over time, you will see a pattern in how business procedures have been able to reduce or completely do away with some tedious manual processes. This is especially true for routine tasks.

Even while this level of automation has been successful, it has been difficult to implement when operations call for systematic adjustments to internal processes, input from outside sources, or variables with variable functional capacities. In general, the machine revolution has proven successful, although this success has generally been restricted to predictable systems and processes.

However, things have changed as a result of machine learning. For specific jobs, several machine learning models are created, guaranteeing that they can aid in real-time problem solutions. To help with decision-making and request execution in this regard, we offer machine learning models that are specifically created to operate with distinct data sets. Task automation has advanced during the procedure.

Today, businesses that operate primarily as software services benefit from machine learning in ways that go beyond industrial automation. Automation has migrated from the industrial sector to the service sector, benefiting customers, business owners, and end users in equal measure.

## Virility and Security of the Network

The issues we confront online are numerous today. Every time you go online, you run a multitude of dangers, including network anomalies, hacking attempts, and other types of invasions. Most of the time, these threats come with no prior notice. Businesses must have mechanisms in place to detect attacks in advance and strengthen their systems accordingly if they want to retain their secure online reputation.

A proactive security system recognizes threats based on a predetermined danger profile, stops the threat from violating its security protocol, and gains knowledge from the threat profile for future use. Without it, the company runs the danger of service interruptions, data breaches, and other security issues in the event that an incursion is successful.

We have algorithms designed specifically for security in machine learning. These algorithms run to keep an eye on the network and immediately spot any unusual activity. As a result, in the case of an attack of any kind, the network is immediately secured.

Any attempts to breach the network should be reported to the appropriate parties by this system so that they can look into it further and, if necessary, pursue legal action.

The beauty of machine learning is that the majority of the algorithms are constructed so that they learn for themselves every time they interact with various user profiles. They correspondingly adjust to the cyber security environment as a result. The system automatically refreshes itself on the most recent difficulties and insights in cyber security rather than undertaking human studies on various security profiles.

## Improvements in Business Initiatives

The goal of machines and automation is to make our jobs simpler, particularly by enhancing the many business models that we occasionally use. This goal also applies to the service sector. Over the years, we have observed a number of industry leaders from various sectors automate their operations to increase their market reach. To be competitive, smaller businesses have no choice but to look for niches in other industries.

lesser companies automate in the same way that big companies have, although with lesser initial expenditure. Only by incorporating machine learning models into their creative methods can this be possible.

There are so many case studies available now that fit this story. Take a look at how two of the most established industries in the world, Uber and Airbnb, have been transformed. Uber and AirBnB use machine learning models to ensure that users receive the most accurate results possible whenever they use their platforms. This is another effective technique to guarantee that users of these platforms have wonderful experiences each time they use them to meet their needs.

When implementing machine learning models to help them empower their businesses, one of the most crucial things that companies must consider is a needs assessment. The goals of the company and the customer's need for value must coexist in harmony. Any company, regardless of size, can use special machine learning models to help guide their businesses in the right direction when these two work together.

## Charge Handling

Today's firms have a constant problem with keeping their balance sheets organized. Machine learning models have the potential to easily eliminate a large number of expense units, hence lowering an organization's operating costs.

The customer service department is a case in point that most individuals may identify with. When it comes to client management, many firms, especially those that deal with a sizable customer base, frequently struggle. Customer requirements, preferences, and interests are constantly evolving. Trying to keep up with this is difficult.

Businesses work hard to guarantee that their consumers may always get effective and quick help. Beyond this, they must stay in touch with them via phone calls, emails, or online chats. This means that companies with a basic customer service strategy will have to spend more money on expanding their customer service departments. In addition, they must pay for overhead expenses, including training, supplies, maintenance, and repairs.

**One area where machine learning is useful is this.**

Many businesses today use **chatbots** and **automated** customer response models to cater to their customers' needs. The business can continue to have a small department dedicated to solving as many client issues as it can. From there, the bots can help clients by pointing them in the direction of the data they require to address their issues.

For the company, this is a cost that might be diverted to other crucial areas like R&D or used to fund other lucrative endeavors.

In addition, clients are no longer required to wait on hold for a customer support representative to pick up the phone.

### Customer Behavior Prediction

Machine learning models stand out for having an ongoing learning process. They engage with clients on several levels during this process, learning as much as they can to help them gain a better understanding. Although each customer's shopping preferences are different, machine learning models can be used to spot patterns and trends and perhaps even provide accurate customer recommendations.

In an effort to make these models as precise as possible at forecasting consumer behavior, they are improved over time. Because of this, data analysts play a crucial role in many firms. Business decision-makers can determine from their inferences why customers favor certain goods or services over others. These decisions are all dependent on data access, which is done quicker and more accurately than it would be by a single analyst.

**Get Rid of Subpar Procedures**

There are corporate procedures that, while essential to the company's prosperity, are nevertheless prone to error. The entry of data is one of them. This is the initial entry point for the data that will ultimately be used to make crucial business choices. Data entry errors will always have a significant impact.

The cost of incorrect data entry goes beyond merely the expense of correcting the mistakes; it can also have negative impacts on the company's reputation for dependability and credibility, which is more significant for their ability to keep clients. You will always find the right answers, but for the wrong problems, as long as you are using the incorrect facts to make decisions. Machine learning models' precision is unmatched by manual data entry. Many businesses are currently reaping huge rewards in this particular area. In addition to accuracy, they successfully manage to save time and money during the process.

Employees may also experience these advantages. The majority of data entry duties are tedious and repetitive. Many workers tend to avoid interacting with them. They are tedious and frequently reserved for interns or other entry-level workers. Employee morale will benefit from the elimination of these tasks because they are discouraging.

Since these tasks are routine and don't stimulate employees, few people are motivated to complete them well. Data entry is one of the activities that most individuals would want to be eliminated from their job description, according to a short poll of most firms. Without it, organizations can concentrate on enhancing worker productivity.

## Increased Sales

How to grow sales and leads is one of the problems that many businesses are now facing. Analyzing the present problems affecting their marketing departments, improving the procedures, and addressing the concerns raised by the marketing specialists would be a straightforward machine-learning solution to this.

Businesses can use the data at their disposal to this goal in order to better understand their target market and reenergize their sales teams. Consider the current clientele, for instance. You can examine their purchasing patterns and the path from product discovery to purchase.

There are a number of lessons that can be taken away from the process that will aid in attracting new clients and retaining existing ones. Businesses can then offer insight into some of their new products and services and make appropriate suggestions based on this information.

Many businesses have benefited from machine learning models in this area because they can learn from the datasets that are already in use by the organization and quickly improve decision-making and recommendations to the appropriate sales executives. This can also be considered by businesses as a potential way to cross-sell or up-sell to current clients.

## Surpass the opposition

A successful company must constantly maintain an advantage over its rivals. This entails figuring out your advantages over the competition and your strongest aspects. This is how you can consistently offer your customers a solid value proposition.

Machine learning has been helpful in supplying pertinent hypotheses upon which you can base significant decisions in terms of competitiveness. Today, it is simpler to give customers personalized recommendations, providing them with the personal touch that encourages them to stick with and support your brand.

## Optimal Workplace Conditions

How to build a healthy work environment is currently one of the topics that are discussed the most on the internet. People already have a lot going on in their lives, so having a work environment that interferes with their mental stability is the last thing they need. Many companies are embracing the idea of a smart workplace, and the outcomes are astounding.

For instance, using virtual assistants has become commonplace in many offices. They have greatly aided many people in increasing their productivity and efficiency at work when properly implemented. Employees are free to concentrate on their primary goals because automatic tasks like meeting scheduling and minute transcription are taken care of.

Virtual assistant models are occasionally improved by engineers, and one of the best characteristics is the ability to reply to voice command notes.

One area where many individuals have benefited is automatic speech recognition, particularly because it increases the accuracy with which the assistant can understand and follow specific directions. Top performance precision is a given, and these models keep improving and becoming more precise over time.

## Medical conclusion

Machine learning is not only used in the corporate world.

This method has been applied in the medical industry to help find patients who could be at a greater risk of developing certain illnesses. These claims make it simpler for medical professionals to identify patients with diagnoses that are correct or almost accurate.

Doctors can quickly determine a patient's likelihood of readmission or the best medication to treat their ailment using the datasets that are readily available. All of this information is accessible in the form of medical records that are kept in an anonymous manner or in the hospital database's documented symptoms that are connected to the diagnosis.

Patients have a better chance of healing sooner with improved diagnosis accuracy, which reduces the need for additional medicine or involved procedures. Therefore, over time, machine learning has helped improve patient health while also lowering costs in the medical industry.

## The Accuracy of Financial Models

Any company that occasionally works with financial models will be able to appreciate the value of accuracy. When creating distinctive business models in the financial industry, you must abide by certain laws and guidelines. Companies and portfolio managers encounter this on a regular basis.

Machine learning models have been used successfully over the years in a variety of applications, including loan underwriting, algorithmic trading, and fraud detection and prevention, one of the most crucial problems facing the financial sector right now. This is an ongoing process that continually recognizes subtleties and anomalies, examines them, and improves. You gain from a precise model as a result, which boosts your company's productivity.

## Detection of spam

One of the applications of machine learning that receives the greatest attention is spam identification. Every minute, trillions of emails are handled. Therefore it's crucial that you get the right ones. Email service providers utilize a rule-based strategy to filter spam from communications before they reach the end user. They were able to use neural networks that recognize spam emails and stop them from reaching the main inbox because of their distinctive filters.

## The manufacturing sector's maintenance

Maintenance processes are required in the manufacturing sector to make sure that all systems function as they should. Without it, the entire procedure would be negatively impacted.

However, maintaining a system can be very expensive, and its effectiveness is not always guaranteed. The entire sector has benefited from efficient, predictable maintenance schedules because of machine learning.

With a predictable strategy, it is simpler to anticipate maintenance needs and take care of them beforehand rather than taking the chance of waiting until unanticipated damage happens. Companies can save money on unneeded maintenance by following this procedure.

## Marketing is driven by data

Marketing professionals have access to a lot of data these days.

All of this data, from lead generation to sales and marketing statistics, might be useful, but many executives are unsure of how to use it. Value prediction is one of the areas where most businesses fail, even with access to as much consumer data as possible. With enough data, businesses may divide their consumer base into several strata that help them achieve their sales goals.

They can take into account things like how many people visit their websites or how well various campaigns are doing in comparison to predetermined benchmarks. Despite having access to this information, most businesses still make decisions based on speculation. Machine learning models replace the need for hunches with a consistent approach to solving the problems at hand.

One of the best examples of this is companies that let clients try out portions of their services before upgrading to the paid version. In order to ascertain the possibility that clients will upgrade to the premium plan, the organization can examine the user activity patterns during the test period. They can use this information to figure out how to communicate with customers in order to understand their choices or even to persuade them to upgrade to the premium version before the free trial period ends.

Machine learning is the force that we must compete with in terms of generating digital innovation. People and organizations who have embraced machine learning are able to find, examine, and comprehend patterns and fresh behavioral trends from various data sets. Automated analytics can be utilized to shorten the majority of typically drawn-out commercial decision-making procedures.

In light of all the advantages of machine learning that have been mentioned thus far, it is important to emphasize that it works best when data is at the center of the business processes that need to be automated. Machine learning is transforming how we do business, connect with one another, and—most importantly—interact with the tools that make our lives simpler every day. This is true for both major organizations and small and medium-sized firms.

MACHINE LEARN

# In-depth Learning

Understanding deep learning might be challenging because it is a very complex topic. If it describes you, try not to be dejected. Read this book quickly by keeping it nearby. You will eventually understand what it means, and if you are sincere about learning more, don't be hesitant to do so. We appreciate you joining us as we explore the fields of deep learning, artificial intelligence, and machine learning.

However, in order to categorize spoken words, Google and Facebook are attempting to identify them. Additionally, they are attempting to assist various machines in assessing the relationship between various variables or data points and identifying the relationships between various objects in the training data set.

For instance, you must find a way to transfer some characteristics of the elephant to more sophisticated characteristics if you want a computer to understand "this is an elephant" exactly in that manner rather than "this is a collection of pixels." For instance, if you know how to change the attributes of that item into ones that the machine can recognize, you can convert a line, curve, pixels, sounds of alphabets, and much more. The output can then be predicted using inference or indexing.

**"Deep learning" is the term used to describe this process.**

Deep learning models use neural networks to detect the outputs. Different nodes are used as inputs in the various layers in this type of learning, and a signal from the input layer is sent to the network's hidden layers. The output will subsequently be calculated or determined by the hidden layers using this input. How the human mind learns defines the work in deep learning, which also takes into account how calculations and computations occur in the cerebral cortex of the human brain.

Each node in the model has a weight assigned to it. **For instance,** you can give each pixel in the input image a weight if you want to use the model to identify or categorize photographs.

The output value that you want the machine to produce should also be included in the training data set. If the output image differs from the one in the training data set, an error message is sent to the input layer or the source. The weights given to the nodes will therefore need to be changed.

The user can direct the network to produce the desired results by altering these weights. The machine is able to calculate the right values that must be delivered as the output thanks to the signals that are passed from one side of the neural network to the other. Deep learning can be used by a system in either supervised or unsupervised mode.

## Monitored modes

A training data set is used to teach the neural network new things. You must supply the values connected to the input category to the output layer in this kind of learning. The network will examine the output layer and give the user the desired output when a similar data set is utilized as the test data set.

## Unmonitored Modes

The examples you're analyzing are supplied to the network's input and output layers. Most of the features in the data set are ignored because the inner, or hidden, layers of the network are compressed. The network will use the values generated by the inner layer as the output in this learning mode.

Since it enables them to recognize the features that a network can support, scientists and engineers are now devoting time to understanding deep learning systems. This aids the engineer or programmer in comprehending how the various data aspects might be combined to get the required result.

Utilizing these methods has the drawback that they are impenetrable. Most systems struggle to find and report on new features in the data set. Since a machine must be able to explain the process it is used, this makes it very challenging for the model to do so. As a result, the model may show you some outputs or conclusions that it is unable to adequately explain. In this instance, you'll need to learn more about the model to comprehend how it arrived at a particular output.

The **majority of engineers and developers use various machine-learning approaches to aid computers in learning**. One of the numerous methods used to assist a machine in learning to accomplish this by doing is deep learning. Cars can now recognize stop signs, pedestrians, and lampposts; it is one of the primary technologies utilized to enable a car to navigate through the streets without a driver. Additionally, voice-activated devices like phones, tablets, TVs, and other hands-free gadgets like Alexa use deep learning. The technology sector can now accomplish results that were previously unattainable thanks to deep learning.

Deep learning techniques are used to train computer models to perform classification tasks using text, sound, or image data. Where humans fall short, a machine using deep learning models can achieve a high level of accuracy. These machines also outperform us. Large data sets, referred to as the training data set, and neural network architecture are used by engineers to train the machines.

**What is the Process of Deep Learning?**

Because most deep learning methods rely on neural network architecture, deep learning models are also referred to as deep neural networks. The network's several undiscovered layers are referred to as "deep" layers. A deep neural network can have nearly 150 hidden layers, compared to a standard neural network's maximum of two. Deep learning models eliminate the requirement for the engineer to manually extract features from the data in order to train the machine by using large data sets known as the training data set and neural networks to learn features from the data.

Convolutional neural networks, also referred to as CNNs, are among the most popular varieties of deep networks. Images and other two-dimensional data can be processed effectively with this kind of network. In order to process the input data, a CNN combines the features it has already learned with the features present in the input data using two-dimensional convolutional layers.

The necessity to manually extract features from data is removed by a CNN.

In order to help the network categorize them, the engineer does not need to classify the characteristics or identify the images. The CNN immediately extracts the features from the supplied data or images. The data is not trained by the engineer to select specific features from the information given to it. When the engineer feeds the training data set to the CNN, it learns what features to look for. Computers or models with CNN are employed to classify items because of this.

A CNN develops the ability to recognize the many elements and structures of an image. It accomplishes this by making use of the network's several hidden levels. Every hidden layer reveals intricate details of the image, and the intricacy rises with the number of concealed levels. For instance, whereas the last layer may recognize various objects in the background, the first concealed layer can detect colors in the image.

# Neural Deep Network

The distinction between neural networks and other ML algorithms in a variety of fields and industries. Let's cut through the hype and examine the true nature of neural networks, how they vary from other machine learning methods, and how they are used in contemporary contexts.

The idea of supporting a neural network has been around for many years. However, in more recent times, its computing power has surpassed the demand. A supercomputer is not required to handle huge computations thanks to distributed systems like Hadoop's MapReduce architecture. Spreading the work item over groups of inexpensive hardware is necessary for neural networks.

Numerous media reports have claimed that artificial neural networks function like the human brain, but these claims are oversimplified. One major difference is the vast disparity in scale.

Even while the scale of neural networks has greatly expanded, there are still only a few million neurons in each network. When compared to the enormous 85 billion neurons found in a typical human brain, this is negligible.

The way the neurons are coupled between the two is the second key distinction. All of the neurons in a human brain are linked to nearby neurons. A conventional network only has one direction in which information can flow. **Information in neural networks is divided into three layers:**

- The **input layer** is made up of neurons that are only responsible for receiving and transmitting data. The features in the data set will correspond to the number of neurons in the input layer.

- **Outside Layer**: The amount of nodes in the outside layer depends on the type of model you are creating. Every type of label you apply will have its own node in a classification system. A regression system will also have a single node that outputs a value.
- **Hidden Layer**: Between these two layers, things begin to take an interesting turn because a hidden layer is present. It has several neurons in it. The number of neurons in the input and output layers will determine how many there are in the middle layer. Before passing the input on, these nodes in the hidden layer will change it. As this network is trained, the nodes get more accurate and predictive, and the output starts to carry more weight.

## The models' training

One approach to conceptualizing neural networks is to picture a black box with several knobs on one side. They are described in this fashion by neural network pioneer Yann LeCun. Let's look at the case of a neural network that we are trying to train to determine whether or not a photo is one of a cat. This is a real-world illustration. The output layer of a model must be trained by adjusting these knobs until it can correctly identify a cat's image. It goes without saying that it is impossible to manually turn all of the knobs when there are numerous knobs involved. The advanced machine learning algorithm comes into play here. These knobs are automatically adjusted by algorithms until the model matches the input data. This indicates that they are altering the ways in which various neurons in the hidden layers weigh things.

Another crucial point to keep in mind is that, in this example, we are tweaking the knobs till we have one excellent dog detector, or we might move them slightly until there is an excellent cat detector. Alternatively, we can reposition the knobs until we have a single, enormous submarine detector. The discussion's main argument is that because the structures are universal, they can be taught to respond to a variety of requests. Because of this, neural networks are more effective. What machine learning algorithms and weighing functions we use is the key to the whole thing.

## Tools & Skills Required

Artificial intelligence and machine language technologies both benefit from neural networks' cutting-edge capabilities. This technique requires knowledge of statistical analysis, huge data processing, distributed systems, and other relevant topics in order to be implemented. Fortunately, there are many libraries that can be used to create and deploy neural networks quickly and easily. These are the more well-liked choices:

### TensorFlow

It is a well-known entry in the field of machine learning and was created by Google as the open-source replacement for DistBelief, the previous framework they used to train neural networks.

This framework uses a multilayered node system to enable efficient setup, training, and installation of artificial neural networks using enormous datasets. This enables Google's voice recognition software to recognize words and locate objects in pictures.

### Scikit-learn

It adds a set of techniques necessary for the typical data mining and machine learning applications, building on the core Python libraries like SciPy and NumPy. Both supervised and unsupervised neural networks are supported by these. The library Scikit-learn has a lot going for it. Its contributions are created by numerous ML professionals, and its tools are properly documented. The fact that it is a curated library is significant since it frees the developers from having to choose between different iterations of the algorithm. Many data-intensive startups, such as OKCupid, Birchbox, Spotify, and EverNote, favor the option due to its simplicity of use and strength.

## Theano

This Python machine learning module evaluates and improves mathematical statements by using a syntax like NumPy. Its usage of the GPU, which is 100x faster than the CPU in handling data-intensive operations, makes it unique. Theano is very useful for deep learning and other complicated computational problems because of its speed.

## DeepLearning4j

The implementation of neural networks, which are frequently used for anomaly detection, recommender systems, and image recognition, is made possible by this Java-based framework. It has APIs that make it possible to utilize the program with more data-oriented programming languages like Python, Clojure, and Scala.

## Neural Networks: Why Use Them?

Large amounts of data are being used by every business to enhance operations. Because there are so many variables in these data sets, it is challenging for humans to understand the patterns that exist there; neural networks make it simpler to find these hidden patterns in the data set. If a computer's architecture does not include a neural network, some computers also struggle to recognize the trends in the data set. Large data sets can be used by an engineer to train the neural network and make it an expert in the subject. The network can then be used to forecast the outcome for any potential input. The engineer now has the ability to respond to some crucial questions regarding the future.

**The following are some benefits of neural networks:**

•They can represent any information given to them during the learning stage.

•Since neural networks can compute some data in parallel, machines with neural network architecture work more quickly to produce results.

•If a neural network is partially damaged, it can cause a drop in performance. However, the network can retain s functionality.

**Neural network types**

**neural networks with convolutions**

Image recognition occurs automatically for humans. It occurs almost immediately. When we see a picture of our grandmother, we instantly recognize her without having to think about it. Anybody can recognize a bird when they see one. This technique comes naturally to our brains, but teaching a computer to execute it is a difficult undertaking.

This is now possible with computers thanks to convolutional neural networks. This neural network employs exact copies of the same neuron. As a result, the network can exploit a single neuron's features in a variety of different ways after learning about them.

A convolutional neural network's architecture is based on the biological process that takes place when a person recognizes something with their sight. Individual cortical neurons in the human eye respond to light stimulation as it enters the field of vision. This area, which is almost totally covered with neurons, is referred to as the "receptive field." This method is carried out using convolutional neural networks (CNN) in a computer.

These networks belong to a unique type that has been improved to become incredibly strong in particular disciplines like image recognition and classification. They are the main component in contemporary technologies like self-driving cars and are capable of recognizing objects, signs, and other cues.

Each CNN has a number of interconnected sub-sampling layers as well as additional layers. When data is input, it is based on a very precise formula that tells the computer the image's height, width, number of colors, and any additional features that will enable the computer to identify the data.

The computer needs to be taught to recognize an object in order to build a CNN. anything. By connecting a number of neurons together, computers can solve a variety of issues, much like with other kinds of neural networks. In this manner, all the neurons collaborate to calculate the pertinent aspects of the issue. With a CNN, you can apply the same algorithms to various kinds of problems. You can make the process simpler by modifying the algorithm to recognize an object rather than coming up with a numerical calculation.

To that purpose, scientists have already produced a dataset of handwritten numbers known as the MNIST, which includes more than 60,000 pictures of handwritten numbers. Computers can only recognize numerical values, not visual representations; thus you will need to convert the photographs into a matrix of numbers that represents the various attributes of the image.

This image must be converted from a visual image to a matrix with more than 300 numbers in order to be input into a neural network. The neural network needs to be enlarged such that it has at least two outputs instead of only one in order to handle all of these inputs. The chance that the image is, for example, 7, will be calculated in the first output, whereas the likelihood that it is not will be determined in the other output. The system will then classify every image in the database, producing a different output for each category of objects it needs to recognize.

The neural network can distinguish objects when correctly configured to do so, but it cannot equal the human eye's ability to do so. This kind of function can be very beneficial in a variety of businesses that require recognizing abilities in circumstances when people are unable to work at an incredibly fast rate.

## Backpropagation and Perceptron

The perceptron is the most fundamental and straightforward type of neural network. It has a straightforward binary function with just two outcomes that it can produce. The function will output a 1 if the result is a positive solution, but a 0 if the result is a negative one.

This kind of network is intended to solve a very particular class of issues, such as item identification. A single perceptron can recognize a line of division and determine whether a given location is above or below the line.

## Perceptron Multilayer

Multilayer perceptrons are frequently used to examine a lot of data that is organized in tables. They are able to interpret columns and rows and use them as variables. When the rows and columns are interchangeable, this approach performs best. They can switch them around without worrying about the data's meaning or value altering.

In an MLP, a nonlinear transformation formula is used to first alter the input for the classifier. The input data is then moved into a region where it can be split linearly. Typically, one of the network's hidden layers is where this is carried out.

Parameters must be set before an MLP can be trained. The characteristics of the classifications that must be formed must be represented by these criteria.

The good news is that rules have been developed over the past few decades that make choosing these parameters considerably easier. Many of these recommendations are already in place and can be found in tools like the Efficient BackProp.

## Comparing neural networks to traditional computers

Neural networks and conventional computers don't address problems in the same way. The former exclusively employ algorithms to address a specific issue. If they know the processes to take to find the solution, conventional computers can likewise solve issues. This means that while conventional computers frequently find solutions to issues that people can handle, they are unquestionably more beneficial when they can find solutions to issues that people cannot.

The network's neurons are linked together. For most issues, the neural networks always cooperate with one another. The engineer cannot instruct the network to carry out a particular task since the network learns via imitation. It is crucial that the engineer carefully select the training data sets because of this. Otherwise, teaching the machine how to solve a problem correctly is challenging. The neural network can solve many different problems because it learns from the data set, including those that the engineer did not educate the system to answer. They are, therefore very unpredictable.

Cognitive techniques are also used by computers to solve problems. When the engineer gives the machine the right instructions, which can be given to it using a high-level programming language, the machine should be able to figure out the procedure it has to follow in order to solve the problem. The instructions will then be converted by the computer into a language that it can comprehend. This method aids the engineer in predicting how a machine will function. The engineer can be positive that if there is a problem with the outcome, it is a hardware or software issue.

Traditional computers and neural networks can work together. While some complex tasks, such as mathematical calculations, are better suited for neural networks than for conventional algorithmic computers, the majority call for a combination of these techniques to ensure that the machine operates as efficiently as possible.

# Massive Data Analysis

Dealing with huge amounts of data is pretty much what it sounds like; big data. And when we say vast, we mean mind-bogglingly enormous amounts of data — gigabytes, terabytes, and petabytes. To put this quantity in perspective, a petabyte is equal to 1015 bytes. 1 PB is equal to 1,000,000,000,000,000 bytes when written out. The size of the data sets handled by Big Data is quite astounding when you consider that a single byte is equivalent in storage to a single letter like an "a" or "x." These sizes are also getting bigger every day.

Despite the fact that computer scientists have been working with massive amounts of data for decades, the term **"Big Data"** only first appeared in the **1990s.**

The scale of data sets started to exceed the capacity of conventional data analytics software, which is what distinguishes Big Data from previous data sets. Hadoop is an example of a new database storage system that was needed to keep the data, as well as new software to be able to handle this volume of data effectively.

**Big Data today refers to a set of presumptions and practices** that have given rise to a distinct discipline in its own right. Most conversations on big data start with the three Vs. Big data is defined as data with a greater variety that arrives in greater quantities and at a faster rate (acceleration would be a more appropriate term here, but then we'd lose the alliteration).

## Volume

The large amount of data that is available is referred to as volume. The sheer volume of data accessible for analysis at the time the phrase "Big Data" was first used in the early 2000s was staggering. The amount of data produced since then has increased dramatically. In fact, the amount of data produced has increased to such an extent that new storage methods have to be developed in order to keep up. The amount of data that is available is expanding geometrically, doubling every two years, and shows no signs of slowing down.

## Velocity

The rate at which data is produced has increased along with the amount of data that is being generated. In addition to producing large volumes of data, devices like cell phones, RFID chips, and real-time facial recognition must also deal with this data as it is being created. It must be kept for subsequent processing if it cannot be handled immediately. The ability of bandwidth, computing power, and storage space to hold this data for eventual use is being strained by the speed at which it is arriving.

## Variety

There is no single format used to produce data. It is produced in structureless text and email documents, numerically recorded in extensive databases, and digitally stored in streaming music and video. Financial transactions, stock market data, and other information are all specially arranged. Large amounts of data must be handled quickly, but they are also created in a variety of forms that require different processing techniques for each type.

**Two additional Vs have recently been added:**

## Value

Data has intrinsic value, but you can only get that value out of it if you can. Additionally, the value of input data is influenced by its state, including whether it is neatly structured in a database of numbers or unstructured text message chains. The more work required before a data set can be handled, the less structure it has. Well-formatted data is more valuable than poorly structured data in this respect.

## Veracity

Not all collected data is of the same caliber. Knowing whether or not the data being utilized is accurate has a significant impact on how much weight is given to the information that analysis of the data produces when dealing with assumptions and predictions that have been extracted from large data sets. There are numerous factors that reduce data reliability. Assumptions made by individuals who collected the data may have influenced it. A data set may have mistakes and omissions due to software problems. Data anomalies, such as when two wind speed sensors next to each other record differing wind directions, might degrade the reliability of the data. There is no way to tell from the data alone if one of the sensors is failing. A company's social media feed contains a number of incredibly nasty evaluations, for example, thus sources can also be of dubious reliability. Were they made by humans or by robots? Human error occurs when someone enters their phone number mistakenly when registering for a web service. There are also a variety of other ways that data integrity can be compromised.

The **goal of handling all this data is to separate useful detail from noise** so that firms can find methods to cut expenses, boost productivity, create new products and brands, and make better-informed decisions. Analyzing the data generated by their population and industry can provide governments with similar advantages.

Almost every machine learning device has the ability to analyze massive data, and it frequently does so in order to produce the outputs that are required. Big data analysis is extremely relevant to machine learning technology, so it's critical that those learning machine learning also take the time to learn about big data analysis. We will study what big data is in this chapter, how it is used, and why it is so important to the operation of machine learning technologies.

**<u>Describe Big Data</u>**

Big data, in its simplest form, refers to extraordinarily massive sets of data that computers analyze to identify particular patterns, trends, or correlations between the information being given in the data.

This data frequently depicts human behavior or interactions, either with one another or with certain things that the data represents. Depending on the data, it may be possible to determine how frequently different demographic groups connect with one another or with different types of marketing tactics, or with certain objects.

Although the term "big data" is relatively straightforward in and of itself, it can refer to a vast array of different kinds of data. Big data, for instance, may include tens of thousands or even millions of demographic details, such as a person's residence, age, and level of education or employment. What illnesses people have, where they live most frequently, and how easily they can receive medical care are examples of additional data.

Big data may also include information about the most popular online pages, the most often opened email attachments, and the most popular social media sites. As you can see, there are numerous ways to collect data, organize data, and sort data using big data.

Machine learning devices are able to accomplish almost anything when it comes to collecting massive data. It can be used to find anomalies, detect trends and patterns, and pinpoint specific trends and patterns that are pertinent to a given set of parameters. This can serve a variety of objectives, from enabling the machine learning device to carry out specific activities independently to enabling it to offer pertinent information for humans to carry out specific jobs, as you will soon see. The device's intended usage, the goal of the big data analysis, and the intended use of the data by the people executing the software will ultimately determine how this information is used and what the outcome will be.

## Big Data: Why Is It Important?

The value of big data is more closely related to what you do with it than to how much data you have. For instance, when it comes to business, you can use data from almost any source and analyze it to get insights that can help you better your company in a variety of ways. This information could be used to aid you with anything from producing new goods, cutting costs, or saving time in your organization to making more informed decisions that will benefit your bottom line.

Big data and powerful analytics can be used to detect fraud before it ever has an impact on your business and assist you in identifying the underlying reasons for business failures or faults almost immediately after they occur.

You may even utilize it to create new coupons or tweak your marketing tactics in light of customer purchasing patterns.

Big data can be useful outside of business in a variety of ways as well. Big data, for instance, can assist governments in determining what matters most to the citizens they are assisting and how to make decisions that will meaningfully advance their civilizations and societies. Big data can be used in schools to help teachers pinpoint the areas where students are struggling the most with their education and introduce fresh teaching methods to improve those kids' learning. Big data can be utilized in the sciences to spot abnormalities in research results, establish novel patterns, and find new areas for investigation. Big data can also be used in the sciences to predict things like new disease strains, weather trends, or specific changes that are anticipated to occur over time in different eco systems.

Big data can benefit many aspects of our contemporary society, from businesses and enterprises to the government and educational systems, as well as the sciences and other fields. Big data is significant because, when properly utilized, it may provide us with the finest insight of what is happening in a certain set of analytics and any potential issues we may be encountering.

This can be used to mitigate negative effects when we utilize it to detect issues that could have an adverse effect on our businesses, societies, ecosystems, or even our bodies. As a result, we may observe a more significant and intentional evolution in our enterprises and communities, which raises the standard of living for everyone.

## Analytics of Data

Due to the fact that big data's primary function is analysis, the terms big data and big data analytics are frequently used interchangeably. A collection of qualitative and quantitative techniques known as "big data analytics" can be used to study a sizable volume of unstructured, structured, and semistructured data in order to find data patterns and important hidden insights. Big data analytics is the science of applying machine learning algorithms and automated analytical approaches to analyze large amounts of data to gather metrics, key performance indicators, and data patterns that are easily lost in the deluge of raw data. The many "big data analysis" steps are as follows:

**Requirements for Data Collection** – Understanding what data or information must be acquired to achieve the company's objective and goals is crucial. Additionally essential to effective and accurate data analysis is data organization. The categories that can be used to categorize the data include gender, age, demographics, geography, ethnicity, and income. The necessary data kinds (qualitative and quantitative) and data values (may be numerical or alphanumerical) to be used in the analysis must also be decided.

**Data collection** – Raw data can be gathered from a variety of places, including social networking sites, computers, cameras, other software programs, business websites, and even outside data suppliers.

Large volumes of data, the bulk of which is unstructured with a small quantity of organized and semi-structured data, are a prerequisite for big data analysis.

**Organizing** and **classifying** data based on the infrastructure of the enterprise A straightforward Excel spreadsheet or other tools and apps that can process statistical data could be used for data organization. Based on the data needs gathered in step one of the big data analysis process, data must be sorted and classified.

Organizing the data, It is crucial to ensure that the data collection is free of duplicate data and errors in order to do the big data analysis effectively and quickly. To move on to the final analysis stage, only a complete data set that satisfies the Data criteria is required. To ensure that only high-quality data is being evaluated and that company resources are being used effectively, data must be preprocessed.

examining the information Any of the four main types of big data analytics approach can be used, depending on the insight anticipated to be gained upon analysis completion:

Using predictive analysis This kind of study is carried out to produce forecasts and predictions for the company's future ambitions. The future state of the firm can be forecasted and inferred from the current state of the company more precisely by completing a predictive analysis on the big data of the company. The business executives are quite interested in this research because they want to make sure that the ongoing activities of the organization are consistent with its long-term goals.

For instance, the first step in deploying advanced analytical tools and apps in a company's sales division is to assess the most important data source. After the believed source analysis is complete, the sales team's communication channels must be examined in terms of type and quantity. The application of machine learning algorithms on client data is then used to get insight into how the company's current customer base is interacting with its goods and services. The application of artificial intelligence-based techniques will follow this predictive study in order to dramatically increase the company's revenues.

The prescriptive analysis is the type of analysis used to improve business performance by concentrating largely on business rules and recommendations to develop a specific analytical path. The purpose of this study is to comprehend the nuances of various organizational departments and what steps the business should do to be able to derive insights from its customer data by following the suggested analytical pathway. This gives the business a clear focus on its current and potential big data analytics process and enables it to embrace domain specificity and conciseness.

**Descriptive analysis:** On the basis of the findings, any incoming data that the organization receives and stores can be examined to generate informative descriptions. Finding data patterns and current market trends that the company can use to expand its business is the aim of this analysis. For instance, credit card firms frequently demand the findings of risk assessments from all prospective customers in order to anticipate the possibility that the consumer will default on their financial obligations and determine whether or not to authorize the credit. The customer's credit history forms the foundation of this risk assessment, but it also considers other influencing factors like feedback from other financial institutions the customer had approached for credit, the customer's income and financial performance, their digital footprint, and their social media profile.

**Diagnostic analysis:** if the name implies, this sort of analysis seeks to "diagnose" or comprehend why a particular event occurred and how it might be avoided in the future or duplicated, if necessary. For instance, social media platforms are frequently used in web marketing strategies and campaigns to gain attention and boost their reputation. Learning from unsuccessful efforts is just as vital, if not more so because not all campaigns are as effective as anticipated. Companies can perform diagnostic analysis on their campaign by gathering information about the "social media mentions" of the campaign, the number of times the campaign page was viewed, the average time spent on the page by a user, the number of social media fans and followers the campaign had, online reviews, and other relevant metrics to determine why the campaign was unsuccessful and how future campaigns might be improved.

## Background on Big Data

Large amounts of data first appeared in the 1960s and 1970s, just as the Third Industrial Revolution was beginning to take hold and relational database development and data center construction were getting off the ground. The availability of free search engines like Google and Yahoo, free online entertainment services like YouTube, and social media platforms like Facebook, however, have recently propelled the idea of big data to the forefront. Businesses first became aware of the vast amounts of user data that these platforms and services were produced in 2005. The same year, the "Hadoop" open-source architecture was created to collect and process these massive data dumps for the benefit of businesses. Due to its capacity to store and extract unstructured data, the non-relational or distributed database known as "NoSQL" started to gain popularity at about the same time.

Companies were able to work with massive data with great ease and at a relatively low cost because of "Hadoop".

With the development of cutting-edge technology, machines, and humans both produce data nowadays. The "Internet of Things" (IoT) and "Internet of Systems" (IoS) smart device technologies have dramatically increased the amount of big data. Our common household items and smart devices are connected to the Internet, allowing them to record our usage habits and interactions with them. This data is then directly fed into big data systems. The amount of data generated every day has grown even more with the introduction of machine learning technology. According to predictions, "1.7 MB of data will be generated per second per person" by the year 2020. Big data's usability still has a long way to go as it continues to expand.

# Tools for Big Data Analysis

Numerous different big data analysis tools are being used by businesses to track and monitor analytics in order to enhance the caliber of their customer relationships and, consequently, their sales. Although it may be difficult to use these tools if you are not immediately clear on what you are doing, they can be used by the average person.

Your ability to apply analytics to make decisions, create strategies, or enhance results based on the data you input into the system depends critically on your ability to work with the appropriate tools.

When we discuss large data analysis tools, what we actually mean is several categories of software that may be applied to huge analysis. This software is extremely accessible to almost everyone and can be used on almost any machine. Having said that, there are eight excellent big data analysis tools available for purchase that everyone can use. Among them are: Tableau, SAS Institute, Sisense, Cloudera, Microsoft Power BI, Oracle Analytics Cloud, Pentaho Big Data Integration and Analytics, Zoho Analytics, and Power BI. We will discuss each product in more depth below so that you can see how these tools leverage big data to serve their users.

## Google Analytics

The main goal of the self-service option Zoho Analytics is to assist users in converting huge amounts of unprocessed data into useful reports and dashboards. They are able to monitor corporate KPIs, find outliers, spot long-term patterns, and unearth several untapped business insights. This intelligence platform is a potent one that may turn business-oriented analytics into fresh approaches to help you reach your target audience and advance effectively.

Cloudera Hadoop technology, an open-source framework used to store data and run applications, is a wonderful fit for larger enterprises that wish to employ it. Larger businesses can easily construct and analyze predictive analytic models for this specific tool by utilizing a variety of tools that have been integrated into this special platform. To use this particular product, you might need the assistance of an IT or technical analyst.

### Google Power BI

Organizations have traditionally favored this particular technology, probably because the Microsoft platform is well-known and dependable. This particular analytics platform is excellent for businesses searching for a simple approach to get started with analytics and use analytics to expand their operations. In addition to providing all of the analytical capabilities built within its software, it also provides cloud-based analytics and, according to the way it was constructed, can carry out numerous distinct types of data analysis and monitor at once.

### Cloud Oracle Analytics

As a self-service company that enables businesses of all sizes to use its platform to create various types of analytics findings from big data, Oracle entered the big data analytics market. This particular tool's main objective is to ingest data and assist customers in identifying trends, patterns, and prediction models that can help them release bottlenecks and raise the standard of their business.

### Pentaho Big Data Analytics and Integration

Hitachi owns Pentaho, another big data analytics business.

This specific business is developed on an open-source platform and focuses on Enterprises. It is great for businesses that use data in a variety of ways, across many different aspects of their operations, and on a huge scale. These businesses typically have large data sources and many different types of data. Because of the way it is constructed, it can effectively manage the more difficult duties and assist larger firms, like Enterprises, in operating better enterprises.

## Institute for SAS

Given its longevity, SAS Institute is one of the most well-known big data tools available. Although it has drag-and-drop functionality, making it very user-friendly, this particular company is frequently used for deep analytics. As a result, it is excellent for creating sophisticated visualizations for the things you want to develop for your company and may help you share that information across many platforms. You can use this tool either locally or through a cloud service.

## Sisense

Sisense is regarded to be a business that makes tracking big data as simple as possible for anyone to perform, regardless of how inexperienced they may be in doing so. Due to its features, it can assist customers of any size and level of expertise in tracking analytics so they may raise the standard of their businesses or organizations. For larger enterprises looking for quick implementation times with a business that provides exceptional customer service, this particular company is great. Predictive modeling and a data visualization service are both included. This specific platform can be used locally or with a cloud-based service, and it can be utilized on mobile or the web.

## Splunk

Splunk is a web-based solution that is simple for many people to use and learn how to utilize. If you work with several employees to watch analytics and monitor big data, you can keep all of your results and comments local in the service thanks to the company's convenient collaboration tools. This enables seamless online team collaboration for entire organizations. For tracking and presenting statistics, this particular organization is well-recognized for producing graphs and analytical dashboards.

## Tableau

One of the top businesses in the sector, Tableau is renowned for being a wonderful choice for scientists who are referred to be "non-data" scientists. No matter what industry you are in, it performs superbly and is ideal for businesses.

It is really helpful that this particular company employs data visualization technology since it can produce data visualization without the user having first to organize the data. This specific platform can assist in the reuse of current talents to enable improved big data discoveries so that businesses can have improved analytics findings.

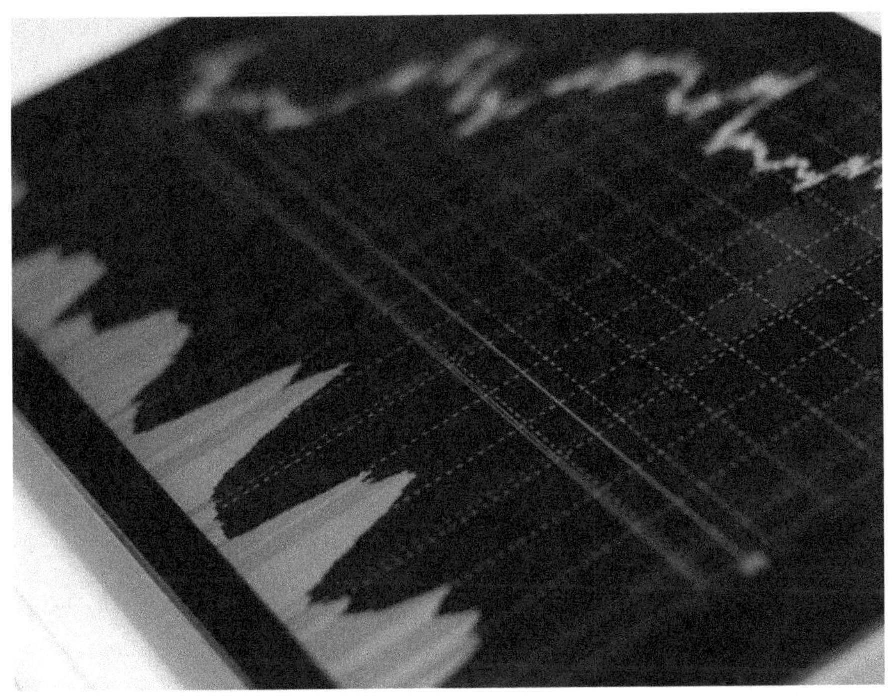

# How Businesses Utilize Big Data

It is crucial to have a full data collection, which big data technology has made feasible, in order to extract trustworthy and dependable information from a data set. More knowledge and specifics can be gleaned from a given amount of data. The future of big data seems bright for getting a comprehensive understanding of a problem and its underlying solutions. **Here are some instances of how big data is used:**

## Product Creation

Customer demand may be predicted using big data. They can categorize essential features using current and previous products and services and then model the correlations between these attributes and their market success. Big data is being used more frequently by both large and small e-commerce companies to understand client requests and expectations. Companies can create predictive models to introduce new goods and services by leveraging the key traits of their previous and current goods and services and creating a model that describes the connection between those traits and the commercial success of those goods and services. For instance, Procter & Gamble, a major global manufacturer of consumer goods, make considerable use of big data obtained from social media websites, test markets, and focus groups in order to prepare for the launch of new products.

## Maintenance Planning

Indicators that can forecast the mechanical breakdown of machine parts and systems are hidden in structured data. Future breakdowns can be predicted using information like the year of manufacturing, make, and model.

**Additionally,** error messages, service logs, operating temperature, and sensor data all contain a wealth of unstructured data. When properly examined, this data can identify issues before they arise, enabling proactive maintenance to be carried out, and lowering costs and system downtime. Companies can increase the lifespan of their equipment by planning ahead for planned maintenance and forecasting potential mechanical breakdowns by studying this enormous data set with the necessary analytical tools.

## Customer satisfaction

Many companies wouldn't exist without their customers. However, in a cutthroat market, acquiring and retaining customers is challenging and expensive. Anything that can give a company a competitive advantage will be eagerly used. Businesses can change and enhance the customer experience by using Big Data to analyze social media, website visit analytics, call logs, and any other recorded customer interaction to gain a much clearer picture of the customer experience. All in an effort to increase the value delivered in order to attract and keep customers. Offers to specific clients can be made more relevant and accurate while also becoming more individualized. Businesses may solve troublesome issues swiftly and effectively, avoiding customer turnover and bad press, by leveraging big data to uncover them. The savvy consumer is aware of all technological developments and only sticks with services that offer the most captivating and improved user experiences. Due to this, businesses are competing to offer distinctive customer experiences by evaluating the information gleaned from customers' interactions with their goods and services.

Making customized recommendations and offers will help you convert more leads into paying customers and lower your customer churn rate.

## Integrity & Compliance

While there may be lone bad actors trying to breach system security in the digital world, the real dangers come from well-organized, well-funded teams of experts, sometimes with the support of foreign governments. At the same time, as new technologies and innovative ways to compromise established ones are developed, security procedures and standards are always evolving. Aggregating these massive data sets speeds up regulatory reporting and helps discover data patterns that may indicate fraud or data tampering. To efficiently identify and stop possibly fraudulent transactions, big data assists in finding data patterns and evaluating historical trends from prior fraudulent transactions. In an effort to stop fraud, banks, financial institutions, and online payment providers like "PayPal" are constantly accumulating and monitoring client transaction data.

## Operational Effectiveness

Although it's not the most exciting subject, this is the one where Big Data is currently yielding the highest value and returns. Reduce outages and waste, as well as foresee future demand and trends, by analyzing and evaluating production processes, customer feedback, product returns, and a wide range of other business aspects.

Big Data can even be used to evaluate how effectively present decision-making processes are performing in terms of meeting demand.

## Innovation

In big data, relationships between meaningful labels are everything. For a large company, this may entail looking at the intersections of people, institutions, other entities, and business processes and using any interdependencies to inspire novel methods to capitalize on these insights. Both new trends and already-existing trends can be predicted and understood better. Understanding what customers actually want and speculating on what they could want in the future are the results of all of this.

The capacity to use dynamic pricing models may result from having sufficient knowledge of certain clients. Big Data-driven innovation is truly only constrained by the inventiveness and originality of those who are curating it.

**Additionally,** machine learning is designed to process large amounts of data quickly. As opposed to Machine Learning, which uses the same data to "learn" these patterns in order to deal with future data proactively, Big Data is focused on leveraging existing data to detect trends, outliers, and anomalies. Machine learning analyzes the current data to determine how to deal with the data that will be collected in the future, whereas Big Data looks to the past and present data. People determine what to look for and how to arrange and structure information in big data. In machine learning, the algorithm iterates over test data to teach itself what is significant. Once this process is over, the system can go on to new data that it has never encountered before.

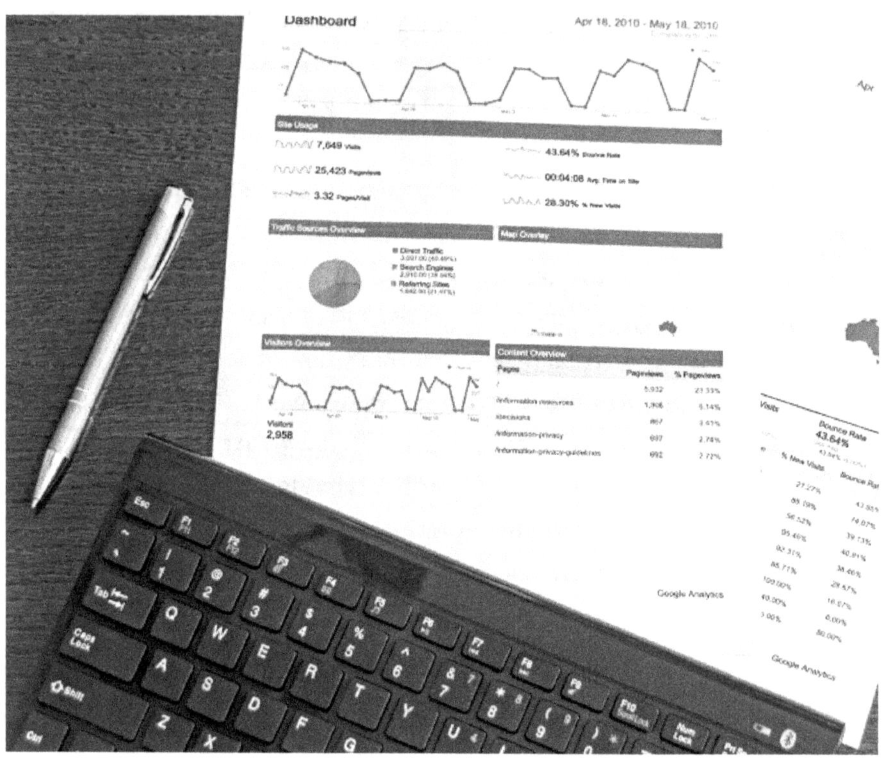

# Analysis of Data and Applications

Machine technology's hottest subfield is data mining. **In the 1990s,** the idea originally emerged. In a broad sense, big data or data science has been used to describe the concept of data mining. Depending on the use and scope, this notion has many definitions. I shall define data mining in this book as the process of removing unprocessed data sets for analysis and the finding of new information about the collection.

The **development of computer networks** has made data storage efficient and affordable. Additionally, the availability of electronic sources has improved data transfer. These factors, along with a number of others, have made data mining techniques more widely used. As a result, numerous firms are able to keep enormous volumes of data in databases without worrying about losing private information.

Databases are very good at storing large volumes of data.

Understanding how to evaluate and interpret the data sets at your disposal is as crucial, though. Large data sets that we are unable to interpret and use to make meaningful inferences are equivalent to having no data at all. This raises the issue of how to examine data that is stored in several databases. The manual hand analysis process was a common technique for data processing in the past. Conventional approaches, on the other hand, have shown to be arduous and time-consuming, with unpredictable results. The analysis processes were flawed since the standard methods overlooked important information in datasets.

Massive data sets have also emerged, rendering outdated and unrealistic conventional methodologies. Automated techniques have been developed to sort data and extract important information, trends, and patterns that may be desirable in order to lessen the issues. Here are some useful data mining methods and techniques.

In plain English, data mining procedures seek to explain an event's consequences, predict future outcomes, and aid in the comprehension of complex data. Data mining has been used to explain occurrences like why a ship capsized, or an airplane was destroyed. In airplanes, data mining is carried out via black boxes that are equipped with datasets and details on each trip. This makes it simple to identify the events that lead to a crush. Data mining techniques are used to anticipate outcomes based on facts rather than intuition, in contrast to other machine learning methods of doing so.

## The procedure for data analysis

The knowledge discovery in databases process, which consists of seven steps, must be followed for data mining to be effective. The following diagram shows the seven steps of knowledge discovery in databases.

cleansing up data. This is the first stage of data analysis. Data is cleaned in this phase to get rid of noise and other variations that could impede accurate analysis.

integration of data. Data integration comes after data cleaning as the next phase. To prepare the data for analysis, this method links, infuses, and incorporates data from numerous sources.

Integration is used, for instance, to combine data that is stored in various databases into a single database.

selection of data. The appropriate group of data is chosen for analysis after all the data have been combined into one file. Data selection is the procedure involved in this.

transformation of data. After completing all of the aforementioned steps, the data is now ready to be transformed into a format that fits. The conversion is carried out to facilitate analysis. For example, some data mining approaches can demand that all arithmetic values be normalized.

**Data mining:** This stage entails using data mining algorithms to evaluate the data and draw out important patterns and information from the sets of data that have been analyzed.

Evaluation of the knowledge and patterns that were extracted. Studying and assessing the information and patterns that were extrapolated from the studied data is the focus of this data mining step. Results might be evaluated in either subjective or objective terms.

data visualization. The creation of the information collected from the studied data is the final step in the data mining process. In this phase, we endeavor to comprehend the result.

It is important to be aware that the aforementioned processes can change based on the method and algorithms employed. For instance, some data mining algorithms may carry out the processes simultaneously or constantly.

## Data mining use in related fields

In the numerous industries and fields where data analysis is essential, a number of data mining methods can be applied. The following list contains a few of these programs.

- identifying fraud
- Stock market valuation forecasting
- Examining consumer purchase trends

The following metrics are used to select data mining techniques in a broad sense.

- The kind of data that will be examined

- The format that the data collected from datasets must take.
- The use of the information (the application of the knowledge).

## Data mining and other research disciplines in relation to each other

Data mining is a cross-disciplinary field of study that includes aspects of machine learning, computer science, soft computing, and other areas. The underlying idea of enhancing artificial intelligence is overlaid by the interaction between data mining and these domains. According to this theory, each branch of artificial intelligence complements the others and functions both dependently and independently.

## Statistics and data mining

Statistics and data mining have noticeable distinctions.

However, there are numerous elements and ideas that are shared by the two research fields.

In the past, whereas inferential statistics placed more emphasis on theory analysis to make significant inferences from the data or create prototypes, descriptive statistics focused more on categorizing data using metrics.

On the other hand, data mining approaches are more focused on the study's conclusion than its mathematical implications.

As long as certain criteria like feasibility and precision are met to the fullest extent, many data mining techniques do not focus on the arithmetic test or meaning. Furthermore, data mining is frequently focused on the automated analysis of datasets, and in most cases, this is done by equipment that can scale to extremely large amounts of data. Mathematicians understand the close resemblance in scope and at times, refer to data mining in statistics as "statistical learning."

## Principal data mining tools

now are a few pieces of software and algorithmic computer programs out now that can help in data mining. The software is used in a variety of models. Some software acts as an all-purpose tool using a variety of algorithms. More specific software is available. It is significant to remember that while some software is created for profit, others are open-source and available for free. Data mining can be done by various software on a variety of data kinds.

Software and methods for data mining have been created especially for usage with various sorts of data. I provide an overview of the many instances of data that are typically encountered below that can be examined using data mining techniques.

Relational databases are the traditional style of database that is most frequently encountered in organizations and businesses. Data is categorically organized in tables in this format. When trying to find information more quickly in the database, conventional techniques like SQL are used to query the database. However, data mining makes it possible to identify complex patterns in the database.

**Customer transaction databases:** These are another frequently used kind of database. Most retail establishments employ this type. All transactions that clients have made are contained in the database. Understanding the patterns of purchase and selling requires analysis of this database. In order to plan their sales and marketing strategies, it enables retailers to comprehend market fluctuations.

**Temporal data:** Temporal data is another common type of data. The commonplace type takes into account the data's time dimension. Here, arrangements are made in a variety of contexts, such as a customer's order of goods, a chain of people who identify as vegan, etc. Time series are created by further dividing the temporal data.

The series is an organized list of numerical data, such as the cost of individual shares on the stock market.

**Data with a spatial component:** This type of data is very simple to evaluate. Aggregate information on the environment, forestry, and substructures like railway lines and air distribution networks makes up this sort of data.

Data that combines the traits of geographical and temporal data is known as spatiotemporal data. For instance, the information could be on the weather, how a wilder beast behaves in a crowd, etc.

**Text data:** The study of text data in data mining has grown very popular. Even though text data is largely unstructured, usage is growing. Text documents lack a clear shape and are frequently unorganized. Examples of text data are used in composition acknowledgment (identifying the author of a specific text) and feeling analysis.

Web data is a category of information that comes from websites. The information is mostly collections of documents, like journals from the web with connections connected. The sets are joined together to create a graph. Some particular examples of data mining operations on the internet include determining the likely next page on the website, automatically classifying the web pages into categories, and measuring the amount of time spent on each webpage.

**Data from graphs:** Graphs are a different kind of database. Social networks, such as the list of Facebook friends, and science, such as a graph of biological molecules and atoms, both contain charts.

**Various data:** A collection of several types of data is referred to as different or miscellaneous data. The classes can be sorted into a particular order and are linked together.

**Streams of data:** A continuous, fast-moving, and theoretically limitless stream of data is referred to as a data stream. For instance, the data stream could contain information about the environment, video camera data, or digital television data. This form of data has a drawback in that it cannot be properly stored on a computer. As a result, the data should be constantly assessed using appropriate data mining techniques.

The discovery of changes and trends is a common data mining activity in stream data.

## Data patterns discovered

As previously thought through, the goal of data mining is to extract valuable informational patterns from data. The following are the most popular designs that can be gleaned from data (please notice that this list is not exhaustive):

## Clusters

The algorithms employed in clustering are always applied in a scenario where data sets are intended to be organized into clusters of comparable instances. These algorithms' primary objective is to reduce the amount of data such that it is simple to comprehend and draw conclusions from.

The clustering operating method favors K-Means and can be used to automatically group students who perform similarly.

## Models for classification

The goal of the algorithms used for classification jobs is to extract models that may be used to classify new instances and objects into groups. For instance, designs that are capable of forecasting patterns in consumer behavior or the likelihood that specific students will pass an exam can be made using classification algorithms like Naive Bayes, decision trees, and neural networks. It is also possible to use these models to make future predictions.

## Associations and patterns

Some techniques are intended to investigate the connection between data and recurring patterns. For instance, data mining methods can be used to examine the frequency of an item set to identify the most popular goods in particular retail locations. Temporal patterns, progressive rules, erratic patterns, and recurring subgraphs are other categories of patterns.

## Analyzing anomalies

The AD is a machine learning technique that looks for errors and discrepancies in a batch of data.

## Easy Statistical Techniques

The easiest method for finding anomalies in a set is to identify the data points that deviate from the distribution of the class of data's mutual arithmetic characteristics. The mean, median, mode, or quantiles may be included in the features. The data with the biggest departure from the central distribution unit, let's say the mean, is the most variable, to put it simply.

Machine learning–based algorithms for anomaly detection. There are numerous anomaly detection techniques based on machine learning. Below is a brief summary of these techniques.

## Detecting anomalies based on density

The K-nearest neighbor algorithm serves as the foundation for this method. In this procedure, it is assumed that deviations are far away and that standard data points follow in a compacted neighborhood. A score is used to determine which types of data points are closest to each other. Depending on whether the data is categorical or numerical, the score can be either a Euclidian space or an equivalent measure. **This strategy can be divided into two categories**

**further;**

1. The K-Nearest Neighbor algorithm classifies data based on matches in distance measurements and is a straightforward, non-feature-based learning procedure.
2. The local outlier factor, is often known as the relative density tactic. The reachability distance metric is the sole foundation of the technique.

## Anomaly Detection Based on Clustering

As was already mentioned earlier in this book, clustering is a key idea in the field of unsupervised learning. The assumption that similar data points tend to fall into the same classes or clusters (as indicated by the distance from the center of the class) is made in the clustering-based method of anomaly identification. The K—Means algorithm is the one that this method uses the most. The K-Means algorithm produces data points in a cluster that have comparable "k" functions. Any data that deviates from the norm is considered irregular.

## Anomaly Detection Using Support Vector Machines

Utilizing a support vector machine is another useful method for finding anomalies. Typically, supervised earning is related to the support vector machine. A few add-ins can, however, be utilized to spot errors in an unsupervised model. The program researches a soft boundary to group the standard data for the training set of data. On the other hand, during the testing step, the computer fine-tunes itself to spot the abnormalities that depart from the learned zone. Depending on the application, an anomaly indicator may produce textual markers or a numeric scalar value for highlighting specific domain onsets.

## Rule of association

A fundamental machine learning theory is association rules. In the examination of the market product pool, the idea is frequently employed. For instance, you will see that all of the electronics are put on the same rack and that all utensils are placed on the same shelf at a shopping mall.

This kind of product organization is designed to make it as easy as possible for customers to find what they need. The layout is frequently pleasing as well, which may serve to remind a buyer of the appropriate types of goods they may be interested in acquiring. Thus, the technique enables cross-selling for the outlets.

The relationships between objects in a large body of data can be found using association rules. It is significant to remember that:

Association guidelines don't go into a person's preferences.

The law does discover the connections between the things in various purchase records, nevertheless. This crucial characteristic sets association rules apart from collaborative filtering.

In association rules, the relationships between the elements are determined by analyzing the IDs of the items that customers have purchased. Then, details in a single group are given separate consideration.

An association rule can be seen in the diagram belowooo. Both the original data and the outcome are included in the layout. A list has every detail. It's important to note that co-occurrence, not relationship, is implied here. Item set is the list of every item in the original set and the generated set for every given rule.

Understanding the degree of the relationship between the two elements can be aided by a variety of measurements.

## 1. Backing

By displaying the frequency of the item set over all purchase records, this measure is helpful. Let's say that the first item set is "bread" and the second item set is "shoe polish." There will always be more bread than shoe polish in all purchase records. The first item set will therefore receive more support than the second because of this.

Item sets with more than one item receive the same treatment. Support, mathematically speaking, is the area of the entire purchase record where the item set appears. developed as: Support (A => B) = Total A and B occurrences in purchase record / Total number of transactions.

The importance of assistance aids in determining which regulations merit further examination.

## Confidence

This measure displays the likelihood that the generated set will appear in a basket that already contains an original set. For example, the measure will typically indicate the likelihood that milk will show up in a basket that already contains bread and butter. In this instance, we will discover that the confidence rule for "bread, butter" => "milk" is greater. According to theory, confidence is the hazy probability that the result will occur given the first set.

Confidence (A=>B) = Purchase history with both A and B / Aoccurrence

## Lift

Lift regulates the frequency (support) of the consequence when calculating the hazard of item B occurring given item A. Lift is regarded as an accurate description of this procedure. Think about this instance.

Lifting that "A" increases the likelihood that "B" will also appear in the same basket. A lift, then, is a rise in the probability of item B arriving in a basket when we are aware that the same basket also contains item A as opposed to the probability of problem B coming in a basket when we are unaware that the bucket contains item A.

Lift (A => B) = (A and B transactions) (A segment of transactions with B)/ (Transactions with A alone)

## Trends and patterns

Data mining techniques can be used to examine patterns and consistency in databases. These patterns can be used, for example, in forms that track changes in the market valuation of stocks and shares and forecast investment outcomes. Other applications are able to identify patterns in how a system behaves and identify the sequence of occurrences that result in system failure.

As was previously noted, the goal of data mining is to uncover patterns in data and draw out relevant information from the designs. Frequency and trends are two examples of events that are crucial to the idea behind data mining. I've always stressed the importance of finding a balance that works for you. The examples provided are merely meant to provide a quick overview of the ideas.

# Conclusion

There are many insights to be gained from looking back at what we have learned in this book. The basis of machine learning is data. Every day, we interact with these systems, scattering bits of data all over the place. Systems learn in this way, allowing for more seamless future encounters and quicker, better predictions.

We approached machine learning from the start in an easy-to-understand manner so that you wouldn't struggle to understand the key ideas. You must comprehend the principles in order to perform machine learning at the beginner level. We walk you through the wonders of machine learning, what you can do with this knowledge, uses, and applications, as well as potential difficulties you can run into as you construct some of the best models, step by step.

With this strong foundation, you not only comprehend machine learning's fundamentals but are also prepared to delve further into its more complex facets. As you advance to intermediate skills and have a better understanding of some of the machine learning algorithms, you should be able to delve deeper into the various models and how to program a model to carry out some basic tasks.

**Although learning about machine learning** is the main goal, you must keep in mind that learning and improving processes is what this discipline is all about. Computers or any other model you construct will accomplish this. The machine will use the information you supply at the moment of contact, along with any provided previous data, to make an accurate prediction of your request. What prevents you from adopting the same strategy to develop your machine-learning skills if computers are willing to learn?

***There are valid reasons why learning happens gradually.***

Don't rush to learn certain techniques in this field. Instead of rushing to tackle difficult machine learning problems and failing, it is better to take your time and master all you learn.

We must also emphasize scalability as a significant factor in addition to the learning component. Make sure to create a dynamic model when creating machine learning algorithms. The environment is dynamic, and so are the data your model will use. This is one of the factors that you should never take for granted when creating models that users will interact with. Many people who do this produce model that never reach the deployment stage.

Think of your machine learning model in terms of evolution when considering scalability. How long will it be until your model is no longer relevant? If you are unable to stop the model from becoming obsolete, you must start over and develop a new plan of action for a different model. A machine learning model that is successful should be able to continuously learn from user interaction and expand its knowledge base. You will need to account for significant computing resources in order to achieve this. You should consider all of this when you are trying to construct your models.

For your models, you don't necessarily require tremendous computational power. The majority of the resources you require will rely on the project's goal. Smartwatches, for instance, have a lot of functionality and can even offer regular health updates to the user, but other than charging the gadget and ensuring that you have access to Internet services, there aren't many other resources required for this.

Machine learning is essentially a needs analysis tool. You need to understand this idea at a fundamental level before incorporating it into your future programming. Don't just create machine learning models because you can or have the time to. Consider the issues you need to resolve, then work to come up with a suitable answer.

Since there are always problems in the world today, you can try to make a difference by using your skills to find solutions. Building a machine learning model requires value addition in the same ways that customers do. Spending so much time and money on a machine learning model only to have it rejected because it works but does no good for anyone would be absurd.

Consider the ease of data access, your ability to handle the volume of data, the services and facilities available for data storage, and, most importantly, the built-in computing power of your devices as you consider the viability of your machine learning model.

You will understand the significance of machine learning once you consider the way in which our world is moving. The Internet of Things is mostly responsible for the information and data that we exchange with our devices. Although this interconnectivity is fantastic, we must comprehend how these systems function in order to benefit from it fully.

We are surrounded by a wealth of data, whether it comes from social networks, blogs, e-commerce sites, or even podcasts. It is crucial that we figure out how to organize this data so that it can be utilized for analysis in the future. Businesses that want to gain a competitive edge must figure out how to combine their operations with machine learning models.

The path to the future is through machine learning. It is a topic of study that will grow significantly in the years to come, whether you approach it as a business or as an individual. Being a part of its growth and progress is one of the best decisions you can make. Many cutting-edge models have been created, and they are having amazing effects on the fields in which they are used.

*Machine learning is quickly becoming an established field.*

Machine learning is not simply being embraced by industrial processes; individual users are quickly adopting the models in all facets of their lives. You must keep in mind that machine learning is the basis of artificial intelligence as we move toward a world where it commands attention. The way we live is changing, and there is a lot more to look forward to in the future thanks to this collection of techniques that draw on historical data and human interaction to learn from experience.

www.ingramcontent.com/pod-product-compliance
Lightning Source LLC
LaVergne TN
LVHW020048160726
843469LV00043B/1563